THE TRIAL OF STEPHEN

THE
TRIAL
OF
STEPHEN

THE FIRST
CHRISTIAN MARTYR

Alan Watson

The University of Georgia Press
ATHENS & LONDON

©1996 by the University of Georgia Press
Athens, Georgia 30602
All rights reserved
Designed by Kathi Dailey Morgan
Set in Trump Medieval and Optima
by Books International, Inc.
Printed and bound by Braun-Brumfield, Inc.
The paper in this book meets the guidelines for
permanence and durability of the Committee on
Production Guidelines for Book Longevity of the
Council on Library Resources.

Printed in the United States of America

00   99   98   97   96   C   5   4   3   2   1

Library of Congress Cataloging in Publication Data

Watson, Alan.
     The trial of Stephen : the first Christian martyr /
Alan Watson.
        p.   cm.
     Includes bibliographical references and index.
     ISBN 0-8203-1855-8 (alk. paper)
     1. Stephen, Saint, d. ca. 36—Trials, litigation,
etc.   2. Bible. N.T. Acts VII, 2-53—Criticism,
interpretation, etc.   3. Jewish law.   4. Roman
law.   I. Title.
BS2520.S8W8   1996
226.6'06—dc20   96-1955

British Library Cataloging in Publication Data available

For Joe Thomson

✛

CONTENTS

✛ ✛ ✛

PREFACE

FEW TRIALS IN HISTORY HAVE BEEN SO MOMENTOUS AS THAT of Stephen. According to our sole source, the Acts of the Apostles, he was the first Christian martyr,[1] his trial set off the first organized persecution of Christians, and it was a decisive step in the breach between early Christians and other Jews, and it was a prelude to the conversion of Saul who, as Paul, was fundamental in shaping Christianity. Moreover, Stephen's argument, if it can be properly understood, should tell us much of what the earliest Christians thought about, and expected from, Jesus.

Yet the trial has attracted little attention except from Christian theologians and visual artists. So far as I am aware, it has no place in any series of "Famous Trials." One reason, no doubt, is that we have only the accusations against Stephen and his short defense speech. More to the point, the speech itself is widely regarded as mainly irrelevant to the charges, with a largely incomprehensible purpose. On the contrary, it seems to me that the speech is entirely relevant. Unique though it is in vital regards, it fits into a well-known genre: those defenses in a criminal trial that do not focus on rebutting the arguments of the prosecution about the facts. Such defenses are numerous and are of various types: a denial of jurisdiction in the court because of the defendant's superiority;

a claim that the law invoked was invalid because it offended against higher law. The most interesting of these defenses share three characteristics that we find in the trial of Stephen. First, their proponents argue or imply that the accused's conduct was justified or needs no justification. Second, they argue or imply that the prosecutors themselves are the real wrongdoers. Third, the defense itself is so surprising that it draws particular attention. Perhaps no topic in legal literature is so revealing of human values.

This book is written on the basis of a claim whose plausibility will, of course, have to be demonstrated. The claim is that in the tradition about Stephen, historical or not, his speech is relevant to the charges against him. The structure of the book is determined by the need for that demonstration. Accordingly, chapters on the meaning and structure of Stephen's speech appear near the beginning. Only subsequently do I discuss other vital topics such as the historical plausibility of the trial and speech, its place in Luke-Acts, and the extent to which textual-criticism has detected conflicting sources of the speech. By leaving these issues aside for a time, I hope I have given my account of Stephen's trial greater clarity. I also hope that my discussion of the speech will have an impact on source-criticism for Acts in general.

One point must be stressed at the beginning. I cannot hope to establish historical truth. At the best I may show the plausibility of an early historical tradition. I emphasize this because of the controversy that has raged over attempts to recover "the historical Jesus." It would be boring to repeat incessantly "according to our source," "the tradition holds," and so on, but I would be grateful if the reader would bear in mind that even when such a phrase is omitted I am not making a claim about what actually happened.

Writing this book and earlier ones on the Gospels has brought me particular pleasures. My first and abiding scholarly passion has been Roman law. And, indeed, without my training in it I could not have written in the way I do about other subjects. But there is no wide audience for Roman law: Roman lawyers write their scholarly works for other scholars in Roman law. Scholars who write on the New Testament are a different case. However scholarly and even original are their theses, they have the potential for a much wider audience. Behind the scholars and divinity students are millions of interested preachers and lay persons, Christians and non-Christians. I have attempted to reach this wider group without sacrificing scholarly accuracy. Again, given the nature of the surviving sources, Roman law studies are primarily about law in books, not law in action. In contrast, law in the Gospels is law in action, although, to be understood, law in books must not be neglected.[2]

This, then, is a book about law in action, and it is certainly not a book about faith. It is also not a commentary on a portion of Acts. Not all issues that appear in Acts 1–7 are discussed: those that I do discuss are treated for their bearing on the main themes.[3]

ACKNOWLEDGMENTS

CALUM CARMICHAEL, BRADLEY NICHOLSON, AND OLIVIA Robinson all read my complete manuscript to my great profit. The staff of the University of Georgia law library were always helpful, especially with interlibrary loans. Sherri Mauldin cheerfully typed many drafts. Elaine Durham Otto, as several times before, was an outstanding editor.

I owe a special debt to my publisher, Malcolm Call, whom I belatedly thank for his unfailing encouragement and aid not only for this but also for previous books.

Indented translations of the Bible are all from the New Revised Standard Version for the sake of consistency, but in the succeeding discussion I use, as will be obvious, my own translation. Translations from the Mishnah are those of Danby.

THE TRIAL OF STEPHEN

1

✢

BACKGROUND
TO THE
STEPHEN
AFFAIR
IN ACTS

✢ ✢ ✢

MY SUBJECT IS THE TRIAL OF STEPHEN AND HIS DEATH. The main problems are these: Why does Stephen who was not an apostle sweep into prominence? Why was the Sanhedrin so hostile to him, possibly more than to Peter and James with whom it also had encounters? What were the charges against Stephen? How plausible do they appear in the historical context? Above all, what is the nature of the defense speech attributed to Stephen? Are the contents of the speech historically plausible? A little must be said to set the scene.

In 63 B.C. Judaea, including Jerusalem, came under Roman domination, but not until A.D. 6 was it placed under direct Roman rule as part of the province of Syria.[1] The main Jewish council and court, the Sanhedrin, nonetheless continued to exist and sit, though its meetings seem to have required Roman permission.[2] From time to time there were Jewish bids for independence or at least revolutionary movements: Judaea was not the most resigned part of the Roman Empire.[3]

The Jews were not united in their views. Most notably, the Pharisees, a self-selected group, believed equally in the validity of the written law given by God through Moses and the oral law derived from it (by interpretation) and in bodily resurrection. The Pharisees, obviously in the time of Luke, do not seem to have shown much hostility to the Romans.[4] The Sadducees, many of whom held high hereditary religious offices, did not accept the oral law or bodily resurrection. Inevitably, those Sadducees who held hereditary office were often collaborators with the Romans: they had high visibility, and opposition could easily earn them death.[5] Another group, the Essenes, had particular concern for purity.[6] For these groups and for the great majority of Jews,[7] especially those who lived in Israel, the Temple in Jerusalem held particular religious significance until its destruction by the Romans in A.D. 70. Only there was animal sacrifice permitted and required (Deuteronomy 12, 16.5).

Many Jews yearned for, and expected, the coming of the Messiah.[8] Not all had the same perception of this Messiah, but apparently the most common and also the most political conception was that as spiritual leader following God's guidance he would return the Jews in exile to Israel and destroy the foreign occupiers. In the eyes of some, one candidate for the position of Messiah was Jesus of Nazareth, who was executed around A.D. 30 by the Romans, by crucifixion, when Pontius Pilate was the procurator.[9] Leading Jews seem to have played an important role in his death by means of the Sanhedrin, though what that role was is much disputed.[10]

Jesus' immediate followers and a few others believed that they saw Jesus resurrected after his burial, and they began to proselytize.[11]

For the very early history of the Christian Church from just after the death of Jesus the only direct evidence we have is in the Book of Acts. How far the history is authentic is not easy to judge, but it does represent the Christian tradition or, at least, the only strand of it that we know. Although we must not leave our critical faculties aside, it is vital to consider closely what the texts actually say and the implications that can be drawn from the texts. When the account in Acts is inaccurate, we have little chance of recovering the truth. One petty example may indicate the scope of the problem: at 6.1 we are told that the Ἑλληνισταί complained against the Hebrews. The word does not recur outside of Acts. At 9.29 it is used with respect to Jews, at 11.20 with respect to pagans.[12] Presumably it signified "people who speak Greek." But with no outside guide, we cannot set the parameters.

I accept the standard view that the author of Luke and of Acts is one and the same and is probably to be identified with Luke, the physician companion of Paul.[13] I shall not repeat the arguments for the proposition. What matters for this book is that, whereas for the life and teachings of Jesus and for attitudes toward him we have four substantially different accounts in the Gospels, here we must assume as a general rule that the author of Acts usually holds the views set out in Luke. To give one illustration of the point, an illustration that has little direct significance for this volume: Mark gives no genealogy of Jesus, never hints that Jesus is a descendant of David, and Mark 12.35–38 should be read as showing Jesus claiming, and demonstrating to the people's joy, that the Messiah was not a descendant of David. Luke claims that Jesus is descended from David (through Joseph!) (Luke 3.23ff.), and its discussion of whether the Messiah is descended from David lacks point (Luke 20.41–44).[14] For Acts, then, we should assume that Jesus is regarded as descended from David.

Still, the evangelist Luke was not a personal observer of the events in the Gospel of Luke or of the beginnings of Christianity set out in the early chapters of Acts, including the trial of Stephen. And I have maintained elsewhere that Mark is closer to an early authentic tradition than is Luke.[15]

For our purposes the starting point for the Stephen affair must be what the first believers—at least as portrayed in Acts—expected from the risen Jesus. Jesus appeared alive (we are told) (Acts 1.3) and ordered the apostles not to leave Jerusalem (1.4). He told them they would be baptized with the Holy Spirit in a few days (1.5). Their response was to ask, "Lord, are you restoring the kingdom to Israel at this time?" (1.6). Thus, on the most obvious interpretation, the apostles' understanding of the risen Jesus was of the traditional Messiah, one of whose functions was to restore Israel to the Jews.[16] In the historical context this meant returning the Jews in exile to the land and freeing Israel from the Romans. There were varying traditions as to the nature of the Messiah, but in the present context we need concern ourselves only with the type found at this point in Acts. What must be stressed is that in Acts this statement in 1.6 is the only reaction of the apostles that is immediately expressed. Jesus talks of their being baptized by the Holy Spirit, and in response they ask if he will restore the kingdom to Israel. As Munck puts it: "The disciples' question sounds as if they had misunderstood the Father's promise and thought it concerned the restoration of the kingdom to Israel."[17] Their response is nonspiritual, but it indicates the importance to them of the restoration of the land and their interest in the Messiah. In effect, the apostles are regarding Jesus as a political leader against the Romans. For Wikenhauser, the apostles regarded God's empire as a lordly renewal of the Davidic empire with the Messiah its king for the benefit and piety of the Jewish people; so they were still captured by the earthly nationalist hope for the Messiah of the mass of the people.[18] I said that the apostles are regarding Jesus as a political leader against the Romans, but I wish to be correctly understood. They consider Jesus as a political leader precisely because for them he is the Messiah. The Messiah regarded politically is the leader sent by God to fulfill God's purposes. The holy aspect of this Messiah must not be downplayed even when it is not at the forefront of attention.

According to Acts 2.1ff. the Holy Spirit descended upon the apostles at Pentecost, the Festival of Weeks,[19] and although they were Galileans they spoke to the many Jews of all nations who were in Jerusalem, to each in his own tongue.[20] The significance of the supposed miracle is not easy to understand, nor was it at the time (2.12).[21] What matters for us is first that the list of nations makes clear that the mission is to all Jews and proselytes, not to others, and second that not all who were present believed (2.13). Mockingly they said of the apostles, "They are full of sweet wine." Peter took the opportunity to preach Jesus as a man approved by God (2.14ff.) and whom the Jews—specifically of Israel—took and crucified by the hands of persons outside the law, i.e., the Romans (2.23). Peter put the blame for the Crucifixion squarely on the Jews of Israel, but equally he insisted that those who repented and were baptized in the name of Jesus would receive the gift of the Holy Spirit (2.38). Non-Israelite Jews will appear again in the story of Stephen, but we may assume that because of the Festival of Weeks more non-Israelite Jews would be present in Jerusalem than was usual. Peter also emphasized that David had died and had not risen (2.29) and had prophesied that Jesus would be resurrected (2.31). Peter is stressing that for Jews Jesus is greater than David.

We should return to Peter's speech from 2.16ff. where he responds to the idea that those speaking in tongues were drunk. Peter explains the speaking in tongues as a fulfillment of the prophecy of Joel.[22] The book of Joel is in two parts. In the first (Joel 1.2–2.27), the prophet regards the plague of locusts that ravished the country as God's judgment on the people, and he calls on them to repent. In the second part, from 2.28 onwards, Joel prophesies that God will pour out his spirit on all flesh; everyone who calls on the name of the Lord will be saved (Joel 2.32); God will restore the fortunes of Judah and Jerusalem (Joel 3.1); all the nations will be judged on account of Israel because they scattered the people (Joel 3.2ff.); the Israelites are to prepare for war (Joel 3.9ff.); Egypt and Edom will be destroyed (Joel 3.19); "But Judah shall be inhabited forever, and Jerusalem to all generations" (Joel 3.20). Joel is prophesying not the end of the world but God's goodness to the Israelites once they repent, the return of the Jews to Israel, and the destruction of their enemies. Peter takes up the book of Joel at 2.28, precisely the point where Joel's second part begins: The Jews will repent, God will pour out his spirit on the people and restore the fortunes of the Jews, God will destroy their enemies, and Israel will flourish forever. Peter then goes on to praise Jesus as being from God (2.21ff.). It is from his Resurrection that the speaking in tongues, and thus the fulfillment of Joel's prophecy, ensue. Though Peter does not say so, he is claiming that Jesus is the Messiah, both spiritual and political, who will restore the fortunes of Israel and drive out their enemies.[23] Luke, in fact, has taken his quotation from the Septuagint Joel 2.28ff. Luke's opening "And it shall be in the last days" (Καὶ ἔσται ἐν ταῖς ἐσχάταις ἡμέραις) has in the Septuagint the less ambiguous "And it will be afterwards" (Καὶ ἔσται μετὰ ταῦτα) Joel was talking not about the end of the world but about the beginning of the new time. Peter in Acts should mean the same because his whole point is that the prophecy of Joel is being fulfilled.

Those who believed in Jesus were baptized (2.41), held all things in common, sold their properties and possessions, and distributed them to all according to need (2.44f.). How complete this communism was is impossible to tell[24] and, as the story of Ananias and his wife, Sapphira, indicates (5.1ff.), there were backsliders. Institutional unfairness in distribution plays a role in the story of Stephen.

One day, Peter and John cured a man lame from birth (3.1ff.), and Peter took the opportunity to address the crowd who gathered at Solomon's Portico.

> 3.12. "You Israelites, why do you wonder at this, or why do you stare at us, as though by our own power or piety we had made him walk? 13. The God of Abraham, the God of Isaac, and the God of Jacob, the God of our ancestors has glorified his servant Jesus, whom you handed over and rejected in the presence of Pilate, though he had decided to release him. 14. But you rejected the Holy and Righteous One and asked to have a murderer given to you, 15. and you killed the Author of life, whom God raised from the dead. To this we are witnesses. 16. And by faith in his name, his name itself has made the man strong, whom you see and know; and the faith that is through Jesus has given him this perfect health in the presence of all of you."

The speech is addressed specifically to the Israelites, who again are blamed for the Crucifixion. Stress is laid on the fact that Jesus was glorified by the God of Abraham, of Isaac, of Jacob, and of their ancestors. Emphasis is on Jesus as a Jew. Stress on Abraham, Isaac, and Jacob will reappear in Stephen's defense speech.

Peter tells them he knows that they and their leaders acted in ignorance and fulfilled what God's prophets had foretold, that the Messiah would suffer (3.17f.). Repentance will cause forgiveness of sin. For Peter, Jesus is the Messiah, and this is stated explicitly (3.20). Jesus will remain in heaven "until the time of restitution of all things" (3.21). It was a commonplace among Jews that the sin of the people would obstruct the coming of the Messiah.[25]

What for Peter is the meaning of the "time of restitution of all things"? In view of Acts 1.6 when Peter was one of those present, we should accept that at least its primary sense is that of the return of the exiles and the defeat of the enemy power.[26] That at least was foretold by the prophets. Thus, for the return of the exiles we have Sirach 48.10 reporting of Elijah:

> At the appointed time, it is
> > written, you are destined
> to calm the wrath of God before
> > it breaks out in fury,
> to turn the hearts of parents to their children,
> > and to restore the tribes of Jacob.[27]

Though Sirach, which was written around 180 B.C., has not won a place in the Old Testament, except for Catholics, its popularity at the time that concerns us was such that it forms part of the sacred writings in the Septuagint—and Acts was written in Greek and refers to the Septuagint version of Scripture—and a Hebrew manuscript of it was found at Qumran.[28] The text also makes plain that before the return of the exiles the wrath of God toward the Israelites will be calmed by repentance. For the destruction of the enemy we have from the first century B.C.[29] the Psalm of Solomon 17.24ff.:

> 17.21. Behold, O Lord, and raise up unto them their king,
> > the son of David,
> > At the time you have [fore]seen, O God, to rule
> > over Israel your servant.
> 22. And gird him with strength, to shatter unrighteous
> > rulers,
> > Purge Jerusalem from the nations that trample [her]
> > in destruction.
> 23. With wisdom, with righteousness to drive out
> > sinners from the inheritance,

To destroy the arrogance of the sinner as a
potter's vessels.

24. With a rod of iron to shatter all their substance,
To destroy the godless nations with the word of his
mouth,

25. [So that] at his threat nations will flee from his
presence,
And to reprove sinners with the thought of their
heart.

26. He will assemble a holy people that he will lead in
righteousness
And he will judge the tribes of the people made
holy by the Lord its God.

27. He will not allow unrighteousness to encamp in
their midst any longer,
Nor will dwell with them any man who knows evil.
For he will know them, that all are sons of their God.

28. And he will divide them according to their tribes
upon the land,
And neither sojourner nor alien will dwell with them
any more.

29. He will judge peoples and nations in the wisdom of
his righteousness.

30. And he will have the peoples of the nations to
serve him under his yoke;
And he will glorify the Lord in the sight of the
whole earth,
And he will purify Jerusalem by holiness as of old.

31. [So that] nations will come from the end of the
earth to see his glory,
Bringing as gifts her sons who are exhausted,

The Davidic king of the Psalm of Solomon is the Messiah.

In this context (3.19) Peter's call to repentance should not mis-
lead: repentance was necessary before the "time of restitution of
all things" could come. This is even spelled out for Peter at 3.20,
and it appears in the text of Sirach just quoted. Peter's message at

this point should still be seen as primarily political.[30] The "time of restitution of all things" should not be taken to mean "the end of the world." Such an idea should not be attributed to the very earliest Christians, the apostles. They await the time of *restitution,* not the time of the *end.* Indeed, the very notion of the political Messiah as he who will restore the Jews to Israel is contrary to any idea of the end of the world, though not to the idea of the transformation of the existing world.[31]

Peter continued:

> Acts 3.22. "Moses said, 'The Lord your God will raise up for you from your own people a prophet like me. You must listen to whatever he tells you. 23. And it will be that everyone who does not listen to that prophet will be utterly rooted out of the people. 24. And all the prophets, as many as have spoken, from Samuel and those after him, also predicted these days."[32]

Moses, like Abraham, Isaac, and Jacob, will reappear prominently in Stephen's defense speech, as will the covenant that is discussed in Peter's peroration (3.25).

While John and Peter were speaking, they were arrested by the priests, the commandant of the Temple, and the Sadducees (4.1ff.). The cause of their ire, we are told, was that, through Jesus, John and Peter taught the resurrection of the dead. The Sadducees did not believe in resurrection.[33] That others, such as the Pharisees, did believe in resurrection might not trouble the Sadducees. But John and Peter were a different case, claiming to have actual proof of resurrection in Jesus rising from the dead. The following day the rulers, elders, and scribes assembled in Jerusalem with Annas the high priest and his kindred (4.5f.). Though to be a Sadducee was to hold a set of beliefs rather than to hold an office, the chief priests were above all Sadducees.[34] The assembly appears to be a trial before the Sanhedrin (4.15).[35] The scribes who are mentioned would be the co-opted scholars in the Sanhedrin who were primarily Pharisees.[36] And the Pharisees did believe in resurrection.[37] Thus, for them, the offense of Peter and John was teaching in the name of Jesus.[38] The Sanhedrin was uncertain what to do with Peter and John because, after all, there had been a notable miracle (4.16). The members told

Peter and John not to teach in the name of Jesus (4.18), then released them. They were rearrested for continuing their behavior:[39]

> Acts 5.17. Then the high priest took action; he and all who were with him (that is, the sect of the Sadducees), being filled with jealousy, 18. arrested the apostles and put them in the public prison.

In the tribulations of Peter and John, the emphasis is on the hostility of the Sadducees, whereas in the Gospels, the main opponents of Jesus are represented as the Pharisees. This, in the circumstances, is what we would expect. Peter and John escaped, were arrested again, and pled, "We must obey God rather than any human authority" (5.29):

> Acts 5.33. When they heard this, they were enraged and wanted to kill them. 34. But a Pharisee in the council named Gamaliel, a teacher of the law, respected by all the people, stood up and ordered the men to be put outside for a short time. 35. Then he said to them, "Fellow Israelites, consider carefully what you propose to do to these men. 36. For some time ago Theudas rose up, claiming to be somebody, and a number of men, about four hundred, joined him; but he was killed, and all who followed him were dispersed and disappeared. 37. After him Judas the Galilean rose up at the time of the census and got people to follow him; he also perished, and all who followed him were scattered. 38. So in the present case, I tell you, keep away from these men and let them alone; because if this plan or this undertaking is of human origin, it will fail; 39. but if it is of God, you will not be able to overthrow them—in that case you may even be found fighting against God!"

Gamaliel's speech is self-explanatory (for the moment), and for our purposes we need not follow the troubles of Peter and John further.[40] But we should note that, at least for Luke, a celebrated Pharisaic scholar—not a Sadducee—who was not a convert might at least express hesitations in disbelief.

In the meantime, the Christian sharing in common was having problems. Ananias and his wife, Sapphira, sold a piece of property but kept back some of the proceeds: the result was that Peter caused their deaths (5.1ff.).[41] But the community's difficulties continued:

> Acts 6.1. Now during those days, when the disciples were increasing in number, the Hellenists complained against the Hebrews because their widows were being neglected in the daily distribution of food. 2. And the twelve called together the whole community of the disciples and said, "It is not right that we should neglect the word of God in order to wait on tables. 3. Therefore, friends, select from among yourselves seven men of good standing, full of the Spirit and of wisdom, whom we may appoint to this task, 4. while we, for our part, will devote ourselves to prayer and to serving the word." 5. What they said pleased the whole community, and they chose Stephen, a man full of faith and the Holy Spirit, together with Philip, Prochorus, Nicanor, Timon, Parmenas, and Nicolaus, a proselyte of Antioch.

Lüdemann points out that the conflict in verse 1 is inherently plausible.[42] Pious Jews from the diaspora often settled in Jerusalem in their old age so that they would be buried in the holy city; hence we would expect there would be many Greek-speaking widows. At that time there were two Jewish systems for looking after the poor: *tamḥūy* 'poor bowl' was distributed daily to the wandering poor and consisted of food; *quppāh* was a weekly distribution of food and clothing to the city's poor.[43] The Christians, it may be conjectured, had a daily distribution connected with the fellowship meal,[44] for their own poor,[45] whether this was in addition to, or a substitute for, the standard Jewish distributions.[46] These verses suggest that the Christian community of property had broken down, if it ever had existed in a pure form.

The Hellenists of verse 1 are not Gentiles but Jews whose native language was Greek, not Hebrew or Aramaic.[47] The Hellenists complained to the Hebrew Jews that their widows were not getting a fair share of the food distribution. There are two possibilities. Either the complaint was justified or it was not.[48] If it was justified, then the Hellenists were discriminated against, and this can only be explained on the basis of a wider discrimination. If the complaint was not justified, the fact that it was made can only be explained on the basis that the Hellenists expected to be discriminated against. In either case, the complaint indicates serious tension between the Jewish Christians from the diaspora and the Israelite Christians. The names of all seven appointed to distribute food are Greek, which probably indicates that Greeks were chosen in order to appease the aggrieved Greek-speaking community.[49] At any rate the apostles took the complaint seriously enough that they set up a board of overseers. Listed first among them as if he were chief public relations officer is Stephen.[50] For Conzelmann, Luke has radically reworked the material to avoid the impression of an internal crisis during the time of the apostles.[51] The tension between Greek-speaking and Israelite Jews has a role to play in the trial of Stephen.

I believe we should not take literally the disciples' remark "It is not right that we should neglect the word of God in order to wait on tables" (6.2). "Waiting on tables" is a rhetorical exaggeration and flourish. What is at issue is the organization of the food distribution, not the actual serving it out at table.[52] Stephen is appointed to oversee the fairness of the distribution.

2

✠

STEPHEN
ACCUSED

✠   ✠   ✠

As we saw, the apostles appointed Stephen to an important role in the distribution of food specifically because the Hellenists complained that their widows were not being given a fair share. Stephen performed great wonders and signs (6.8)—we are not told what they were—but he ran into opposition with members of the synagogue of the Freedmen, Cyrenians, Alexandrians, of those from Cilicia and Asia. *Synagogue* is singular in the Greek, and we should probably take it that members of only one synagogue were involved, namely, that of Greek-speaking Jews.[1] The "freedmen" were presumably descendants of those Jews who had been enslaved by Pompey.[2] Those shocked by Stephen would not be the Christian Hellenists mentioned at 6.1 but unconverted Greek-speaking Jews. Presumably, Stephen used his role of making sure that food distribution was fair with specific reference to the Hellenists to preach his message to the unconverted Greek-speaking Jews. The food distribution—as so often in history—was used as an incentive to conversion. Those who were not converted were angered by the interference with their congregation.[3] Loisy, who is among those who most believe that the original tradition and source have been much altered, thinks that the story of the Stephen affair has been as badly prepared as possible. In his view, the reader cannot understand how someone attached to the "table-service" could become a more audacious preacher than any of the Twelve and occasion much more violent opposition. If my approach is correct, there is no problem. "Table-service," not to be understood literally as waiting on tables, was an important job, and Stephen had used it to carry a war right into the enemy's camp, with tactics that would seem to opponents to be underhanded. Strangely for his argument, Loisy reasonably observes that the propaganda of the first disciples was not in the broad light of day whereas Stephen carried Jesus into the official reunions of the Jews, a bold act that caused him to become the first Christian martyr.[4] Also, Stephen's supposed claims that Jesus would destroy the Temple and change the law may not have been standard among early Christians. This point will surface again.

Haenchen feels that the difference of language "cannot have been the reason why Stephen's group was persecuted." Certainly, the initial anger against Stephen cannot have been because he spoke in Greek: that was also the language of the Hellenists who opposed him. Also, apart from anything else, the appointment of seven Greeks by the apostles to oversee the food distribution must have been a conciliatory act. But Haenchen seems to have gone astray. He continually stresses that "Stephen's group" was persecuted, but there is no warrant for this. It was Stephen, and not a group, who was arrested and tried. One cannot, as Haenchen does, seek to find the reason for persecution in teaching by the group but in Stephen's behavior. One cannot postulate that for many Jews the teaching of Greek-speaking Christians went "beyond the bounds of the tolerable" or that they exercised "great freedom in relation to the law." It is only after the death of Stephen that one can talk of persecution of a group. And that group was not "Stephen's group" but the Christians in general (8.1ff.).[5]

In contrast to Peter and John's healing of the man lame from birth, no specific miracle is attributed to Stephen. Presumably, Luke or his sources knew of none. Bihler observes that the miracles are not stressed, but Stephen's speaking ability is.[6] The cause of hostility to him was not his miracles but his teaching.[7] Stephen bested his opponents in argument (6.10).

Acts 6.11. Then they secretly instigated some men to say, "We have heard him speak blasphemous words against Moses and

God." 12. They stirred up the people as well as the elders and the scribes; then they suddenly confronted him, seized him, and brought him before the council. 13. They set up false witnesses who said, "This man never stops saying things against this holy place and the law; 14. for we have heard him say that this Jesus of Nazareth will destroy this place and will change the customs that Moses handed on to us." 15. And all who sat in the council looked intently at him, and they saw that his face was like the face of an angel.

They suborned witnesses who claimed they heard Stephen make blasphemous statements against Moses and against God. Whether the words were technically blasphemy I shall discuss later in this chapter. Thus, they excited the people and the elders and the scribes. In contrast to the charges against Peter and John, this time the scribes (i.e., Pharisees) are expressly named as hostile, but the Sadducees are not. Stephen's words seem to be objectionable primarily to a different group. The issue was broader than bodily resurrection.

Stephen was taken before the Sanhedrin, and his opponents set up false witnesses, we are told, who said, "This man never stops speaking blasphemous words against this holy place and the law. For we have heard him say that this Jesus of Nazareth will destroy this place and will change the customs which Moses delivered to us." But the witnesses can scarcely have been false.[8] First, Stephen's defense speech, as we shall see in subsequent chapters, makes sense only if Stephen had made such claims. Second the witnesses would have defeated their own case by overkill with the charge that Stephen "never stops" saying these things. There would have been any number of persons who had listened to him and could have testified they had never heard him say anything of the kind. Third, it is entirely plausible as I shall now argue that Stephen believed Jesus had changed the laws of Moses and would destroy the Temple.

With regard to Jesus' changing the law of Moses, perhaps the most obvious example is his declaration that all food is clean (Mark 7.17ff.; Matthew 15.10ff.). Jesus thus pronounced against God's express and very detailed command in Leviticus 11, which was mediated through Moses. In fact, God's command against unclean food was expressed in extreme language: the food is "detestable" or "abominable" (Leviticus 11.10ff.). It should also be stressed that the partaker's uncleanliness cannot be cleansed by any purificatory rite or the passage of time. Moreover, what we have here is not a case where the uncleanliness is discovered by interpretation: God's prohibition in Scripture is explicit. So Jesus' position was opposed to that of both Pharisee and Sadducee. Second, Moses allowed divorce (Deuteronomy 24.1ff.), but Jesus at Mark 10.2ff. condemned it. (In Matthew 19.1ff., especially at verse 9, Jesus seems to permit divorce, but only on account of adultery by the wife.) Modern scholars sometimes claim that Jesus was not changing the law here, because Moses had not compelled divorce.[9] The argument is false. There is a vast legal difference between a system that permits divorce and one that refuses to recognize it. Further, Jesus defended his disciples for plucking grain—working—on the Sabbath (Mark 2.23ff.). God, through Moses, had forbidden work on the Sabbath (Exodus 16.25f., 31.15, 35.2). The express divine prohibition lacks specificity, but Scripture (Exodus 16.25f.) in effect forbade reaping on the Sabbath,[10] and by reasonable Pharisaic interpretation plucking grain was reaping. The rule being based on Scriptural law was thus *halakah:* that is, a legal rule either based directly on Scripture or derived from Scripture by an accepted mode of reasoning. Jesus' reply was not to the point and would not be persuasive to the Pharisees. His legalistic response was that there was a precedent: David and his companions once ate the consecrated bread. But this behavior did not constitute a legal rule, was not *halakah* but was an example, that is, a matter of religious importance which did not affect the law. It was thus *haggadah* which could not prevail over *halakah.*[11] Besides, the precedent was not in point: it did not concern a breach of the Sabbath. And what was permitted to David need not have been permitted to others. On other occasions, too, Jesus showed himself careless of Pharisees' sensitivity to working on the Sabbath, most notably when he cured the withered hand (Mark 3.1ff.). Jesus was there being watched to see whether he would cure a withered hand on the Sabbath. He asked, "Is it lawful to do good or harm on the Sabbath, to save life or to kill?" The question was palpably unfair. There was no prohibition on doing good on the Sabbath, only on working. Even more to the point, even for the Pharisees it was lawful to work on the Sabbath in order to save life, even if there was only doubt as to whether life was in danger.[12] That Jesus then cured without working would not greatly reduce this indignation.

Jesus' offenses against the law of Moses mentioned so far would upset the Pharisees more than other Jews because they were the most rigorous in their observance of the law, both that expressed to Moses and that discovered by interpretation.[13] Hence, I suggest, the scribes/Pharisees played a prominent role in Stephen's arrest, and the Sadducees are not mentioned. Still, the Sadducees, the Pharisees, and all observing Jews alike who did not accept that Jesus was the Messiah would be horrified by his violent affront to the law in the so-called cleansing of the Temple.[14]

The so-called cleansing of the Temple is told in Mark 11.15ff. in a way that is much more muted than in John 2.13ff. Still, Jesus' atrocity toward Pharisees, Sadducees, and all observing Jews alike shines through. Jesus threw out those buying and selling in the Temple precincts (11.15). But the sales, as we know from John (2.14ff.), were of the sacrificial animals: cattle, sheep, and doves for the poor. The sale of such was permitted there by the Temple authorities—indeed the sale of doves was directly under their control.[15] Only religiously clean animals could be offered for sacrifice, and apart from sales in the Temple precincts such beasts would not be easy to find, especially not by pilgrims who had come to Jerusalem for the festival and who did not know their way around. God, moreover, had centralized worship, and sacrifice could be offered only in one place, Jerusalem (Deuteronomy 12, 16.5f.). Thus, Jesus was inhibiting the necessary sacrifices to God, at the one place where they were permitted, indeed, commanded, and just before Passover, the holiest day of the Jewish year.

Jesus also overturned the tables of the money changers. Their function was religious or quasi-religious: to enable the Temple tax to be paid. Roman denarii with the portrait of Tiberius on the obverse, and the graven image of a false deity—Pax in the form of Tiberius' mother, Livia—on the reverse could not be offered. Similar objections applied to Greek didrachms. The money changers gave unobjectionable Tyrian coinage in exchange. So Jesus was preventing the payment of the Temple tax.[16]

The account of the cleansing of the Temple is most specific in John where it occurs, implausibly, at the beginning of Jesus' ministry and, astonishingly, has no adverse consequences for him.[17] In the Synoptics it occurs at the end of Jesus' ministry and not surprisingly leads to his death. Still, it is in this context for all four Gospels that we should place the other accusation against Stephen, that he claimed Jesus would destroy the Temple. That such a charge would be brought is entirely understandable.

In all three Synoptic Gospels, shortly after the cleansing of the Temple Jesus said something that could be interpreted as meaning he would destroy the Temple.

> Mark 13.1. As he came out of the temple, one of his disciples said to him, "Look, Teacher, what large stones and what large buildings!" 2. Then Jesus asked him, "Do you see these great buildings? Not one stone will be left here upon another; all will be thrown down."[18]

Jesus does not indicate by whom the Temple would be thrown down. One assumption of his meaning could be that he intended to do so himself. Such an interpretation would seem all the more reasonable because to those who were not his followers the "cleansing" would be an act of great hostility to the Temple. A rather different version, perhaps less susceptible to that interpretation, is in John 2.18:

> The Jews then said to him, "What sign can you show us for doing this?" 19. Jesus answered them, "Destroy this temple and in three days I will raise it up." 20. The Jews then said, "This temple has been under construction for forty-six years, and will you raise it up in three days?" 21. But he was speaking of the temple of his body. 22. After he was raised from the dead, his disciples remembered that he had said this; and they believed the scripture and the word that Jesus had spoken.

That Jesus was regarded as threatening the Temple appears at his trial:

> Mark 14.57. Some stood up and gave false testimony against him, saying, 58. "We heard him say, 'I will destroy this temple

that is made with hands, and in three days I will build another, not made with hands.'" 59. But even on this point their testimony did not agree. 60. Then the high priest stood up before them and asked Jesus, "Have you no answer? What is it that they testify against you?" 61. But he was silent and did not answer.

Even if we believe that the testimony against Jesus was false it was plausible. Indeed, people did accept that accusation as true. Thus, when he was on the cross,

> Mark 15.29. Those who passed by derided him, shaking their heads and saying, "Aha! You who would destroy the temple and build it in three days, 30. save yourself, and come down from the cross!"

How widespread was the notion that Jesus said he would destroy the Temple appears from the apocryphal Gospel of Thomas, probably written in the middle of the second century, at 71: "Jesus said, 'I shall destroy this house and no one will be able to build it again.'"[19] Thus, even a Christian source could claim that Jesus would destroy the Temple in such a way that it could never be rebuilt. In these circumstances it is plausible that Stephen did declare that Jesus would destroy the Temple.

The charges against Stephen were serious. The law of Moses was, and is, central to Judaism. That law is very wide-ranging. But the charge against Stephen should be seen specifically in the context of Jesus' apparent breaches or neglect of the law: his hostility to the prohibition of working on the Sabbath, to laws or customs of purification, to dietary restrictions, to sacrifice in the Temple, and to the payment of the Temple tax.[20] The emphasis in Jewish tradition on these topics is well brought out by the amount of detail in the tractates of the Mishnah, all the more because after the destruction of the Temple in A.D. 70 the law relating to sacrifices was obsolete but is nonetheless retained. What these rules have in common is that they concern the very matters that in the annual round of life show a Jew that he is a Jew. This would be all the more important when, as at that time, Judaea and Jerusalem were under foreign (Roman) rule. In so far as this part of the accusation against Stephen relates to his opposition to these laws, he was accused of subverting the very heart of Judaism.[21]

The second part of the accusation, that Jesus would destroy the Temple, was no less serious. Through Moses, God had centralized sacrifice and forbade it elsewhere:

> Deuteronomy 12.13. Take care that you do not offer your burnt offerings at any place you happen to see. 14. But only at the place that the Lord will choose in one of your tribes—there you shall do everything I command you.

> Deuteronomy 16.5. You are not permitted to offer the passover sacrifice within any of your towns that the Lord your God is giving you. 6. But at the place that the Lord your God will choose as a dwelling for his name, only there shall you offer the passover sacrifice, in the evening at sunset, the time of day when you departed from Egypt.

The site of this sacrifice was taken generally to be in Jerusalem at the Temple. Indeed, so seriously was this approach taken that one reason for the breach between Jews and Samaritans was that the latter regarded Mount Gerizim as the holy place for sacrifice.[22] The holiness of the Temple is set out in Mishnah Kelim 1.8ff.:

> Within the wall [of Jerusalem] is still more holy, for there [only] they may eat the Lesser Holy Things and the Second Tithe. The Temple Mount is still more holy, for no man or woman that has a flux, no menstruant, and no woman after childbirth may enter therein. The Rampart is still more holy, for no Gentiles and none that contracted uncleanness from a corpse may enter therein. The Court of the Women is still more holy, for none that had immersed himself the selfsame day [because of uncleanness] may enter therein, yet none would thereby become liable to a Sin-offering. The Court of the Priests is still more holy, for Israelites may not enter therein save only when they must perform the laying on of hands, slaughtering, and waving. 9. Between the Porch and the Altar is still more holy, for none that has a blemish or whose hair is unloosed may enter there.

The Sanctuary is still more holy, for none may enter therein with hands and feet unwashed. The Holy of Holies is still more holy, for none may enter therein save only the High Priest on the Day of Atonement at the time of the [Temple-] service. R. Jose said: In five things is the space between the Porch and the Altar equal to the Sanctuary: for they may not enter there that have a blemish, or that have drunk wine, or that have hands and feet unwashed, and men must keep far from between the Porch and the Altar at the time of burning the incense.[23]

According to Philo the penalty for breach of the rule forbidding entry to the Holy of Holies, even by the high priest, was death (*Embassy to Gaius* 307):

And if any priest, to say nothing of the other Jews, and not merely one of the lowest priests but of those who are ranked directly below the chief, goes in either by himself or with the High Priest, and further even if the High Priest enters on two days in the year or thrice or four times on the same day death without appeal is his doom. So greatly careful was the lawgiver to guard the inmost sanctuary, the one and only place which he wished to keep preserved untrodden and untouched.[24]

Josephus even tells us that the Roman occupiers allowed the Jews to put to death non-Jews, including Roman citizens, who passed the barrier.[25]

The Jews' love for the Temple is demonstrated by Josephus in *Antiquities* 18.261ff. To their horror, the emperor Caligula proposed to set up a statue of himself there and sent Petronius to Judaea as his legate. The Jews strongly voiced their determination not to transgress the law. Josephus records at *Antiquities* 18.269ff.:

Now Petronius saw from their words that their spirit was not easily to be put down and that it would be impossible for him without a battle to carry out Gaius' behest and set up his image. Indeed there would be great slaughter. Hence he gathered up his friends and attendants and hastened to Tiberias, for he wished to take note of the situation of the Jews there. 270. The Jews, though they regarded the risk involved in war with the Romans as great, yet adjudged the risk of transgressing the Law to be far greater. As before, many tens of thousands faced Petronius on his arrival at Tiberias. 271. They besought him by no means to put them under such constraint nor to pollute the city by setting up a statue. "Will you then go to war with Caesar," said Petronius, "regardless of his resources and of your own weakness?" "On no account would we fight," they said, "But we will die sooner than violate our laws." And falling on their faces and baring their throats, they declared that they were ready to be slain. 272. They continued to make these supplications for forty days. Furthermore, they neglected their fields, and that, too, though it was time to sow the seed. For they showed a stubborn determination and readiness to die rather than to see the image erected.

Caligula's death finally settled the issue.[26]

The full enormity of the crimes with which Stephen was charged emerges clearly from Mishnah Aboth 1.2.:

Simeon the Just was one of the remnants of the Great Synagogue. He used to say: By three things is the world sustained: by the Law, by the [Temple-]service, and by deeds of loving kindness.

Stephen was charged with wishing the destruction of two of the three things on which the world stands. Neglect of the third, performing deeds of loving kindness, could scarcely give rise to a criminal charge. Though the Mishnah was compiled after the destruction of the Temple, Simeon the Righteous is much earlier, whether he is Simeon I favored by Josephus or Simeon II favored in Sirach.[27]

It should, of course, be noted that not all Jews were devoted to the Temple.[28] Most noticeably, the prophet Isaiah—to whom Jesus bears a striking resemblance[29]—declared the Temple unnecessary, perhaps even wicked, and was hostile to animal sacrifice (which inevitably involved the Temple).[30] A different strand of hostility is found in Philo *On the Cherubim* 99ff.: "Shall we prepare for him

[God] a house of stone or of materials of wood? Away! Such an idea is not holy" (100).[31] Such a view—and it is an important view—is more likely to be found among Jews of the diaspora than among those who chose to live in Jerusalem. Here the miracle of Pentecost is illuminating:

> Acts 2.1. When the day of Pentecost had come, they were all together in one place. 2. And suddenly from heaven there came a sound like the rush of a violent wind, and it filled the entire house where they were sitting. 3. Divided tongues, as of fire, appeared among them, and a tongue rested on each of them. 4. All of them were filled with the Holy Spirit and began to speak in other languages, as the Spirit gave them ability.
>
> 5. Now there were devout Jews from every nation under heaven living in Jerusalem. 6. And at this sound the crowd gathered and was bewildered, because each one heard them speaking in the native language of each. 7. Amazed and astonished, they asked, "Are not all these who are speaking Galileans? 8. And how is it that we hear, each of us, in our own native language? 9. Parthians, Medes, Elamites, and residents of Mesopotamia, Judea and Cappadocia, Pontus and Asia, 10. Phrygia and Pamphylia, Egypt and the parts of Libya belonging to Cyrene, and visitors from Rome, both Jews and proselytes, 11. Cretans and Arabs—in our own languages we hear them speaking about God's deeds of power."

Thus, Jews from all over the diaspora had come to live in Jerusalem, whether temporarily or permanently. And we are to understand, I believe, that their command of Aramaic was imperfect, so they would suffer some inconveniencies in Jerusalem. Why had they come? The obvious answer, I suggest, was to be near the Temple (and by that I mean the physical place) because of the central role it played in their worship. The Essenes, in contrast, may at first sight seem ambivalent. They accepted the idea of a place of central worship in Jerusalem but disapproved of some priestly notions of purity and sacrifice. They sent voluntary offerings to the Temple but did not partake in sacrificial worship.[32] Their attitude, however, is most likely to be based on particular reverence for the Temple and what they regarded as priestly abuses. Out of respect for the holy city, they did not reside in Jerusalem. The standard attitude of Jews who lived in Jerusalem was of extreme reverence of the Temple, and, be it not forgotten, Stephen's trial and the activities around it happened in Jerusalem.

The seriousness of the charge against Stephen that he claimed Jesus would destroy the Temple—and hence also against Jesus— is underscored if we give weight to a passage in the third Jewish Sibylline Oracle. That work is a composite, from Egypt, and the passage that concerns us is the main oracle that seems to have been written around 163–145 B.C.[33] What we do not know is how widely the work circulated and how well it was known, but in general its contents correspond to other known writings.[34] God, it relates, will send a king who, following God's wishes, will stop wars (652ff.). Then comes our passage (657ff.):

> The Temple of the great God (will be) laden with very beautiful
>   wealth,
> gold, silver, and purple ornament,
> and earth [will be] productive and sea full
> of good things. And kings will begin
> to be angry with each other, requiting evils with spirit.
> Envy is not good for wretched mortals.
> But again the kings of the peoples will launch an attack
> together against this land, bringing doom upon themselves,
> for they will want to destroy the Temple of the great God
> and most excellent men when they enter the land.
> The abominable kings, each one with his throne
> and faithless people, will set them up around the city.
> And God will speak, with a great voice,
> to the entire ignorant empty-minded people, and
> judgment will come upon them from the great God, and all will
>   perish
> at the hand of the Immortal.

So, other kings would launch an attack on Israel and seek to destroy the Temple. But they will fail, and God will wipe them out. For those who followed this prophecy, Jesus, as represented by Stephen, would be one of those who sought to destroy the Temple, and he was killed and his followers would be also.

Though we are informed of the behavior—his teaching—that caused Stephen to be accused, we are not told directly the nature of the criminal offense with which he was charged. In one sense the issue is not too significant for our purposes: Stephen after all was finally lynched, not executed, after the trial broke up in uproar. There is no issue here of whether the punishment was that precisely established for the crime. In another sense it is appropriate to attempt to establish that Stephen was properly charged with a serious crime. That is especially the case if the crime was one that entailed the death penalty, more especially if that penalty was death by stoning. Then the failure in conduct of the Sanhedrin might relate primarily to an extremely gross breach of procedure.

The only internal evidence that we have from Acts indicates that the crime charged was blasphemy. Before his arrest witnesses claimed, "We have heard him speaking blasphemous words against Moses and God" (6.11). In front of the Sanhedrin witnesses declared, "This man does not cease speaking blasphemous words against this holy place and the law" (6.13). A different approach, also indicating that the charge was blasphemy, might be suggested: Stephen cursed God the king, that is, the Temple's sovereign, and Moses was his earthly counterpart. But there is no immediate textual support for this approach. Further evidence of the charge is lacking, and it is not conclusive. There is, in fact, a problem. According to the (admittedly much later) Mishnah[35] in tractate Sanhedrin 7.5, blasphemy is solely committed by uttering the name of God. And the Greek words that give rise to our *to blaspheme, blasphemy*, and (in the present context) *blasphemous words*, have wider meanings than our words. They may be used to refer not only to insults to a deity but also to ordinary defamation or insult.[36] The way to advance, I believe, is indirectly and above all by examining the nature of the crime Jesus was charged with.[37] At Mark 14.64, after Jesus had admitted to being the Messiah, the High Priest said "ἠκούσατε τῆς βλασφημίας" you have heard his blasphemy. In

Matthew 26.65, the word is ἐβλασφήμησεν he blasphemed. Much earlier, he was also regarded as blaspheming. Thus, when he said to the paralyzed man that his sins were forgiven, the scribes who were present thought he blasphemed (Mark, 2.5ff.). No other charge at the trial of Jesus is mentioned.

Moreover, the death that Jesus expected was by stoning (Matthew 23.37; Luke 13.34), and this was the penalty established for particular crimes, including blasphemy:

> Mishnah Sanhedrin 7.4. These are they that are to be stoned: he that has connexion with his mother, his father's wife, his daughter-in-law, a male, or a beast, and the woman that suffers connexion with a beast, and the blasphemer and the idolater, and he that offers any of his seed to Molech, and he that has a familiar spirit and the soothsayer, and he that profanes the Sabbath, and he that curses his father or his mother, and he that has connexion with a girl that is betrothed, and he that beguiles [others to idolatry], and he that leads [a whole town] astray, and the sorcerer and a stubborn and rebellious son.

None of these other crimes for which stoning was the accepted penalty would seem to be appropriate except perhaps leading a town astray, but even that is closely connected with blasphemy. Second, it is blasphemy and only blasphemy that is mentioned in the context of the trial, so it should be presumed that this was in fact the charge. Third, it is as the reason for conviction that Mark and Matthew have the high priest say (in Greek) that Jesus blasphemed; it is most unlikely that the tradition behind the Gospels should report him using that terminology untechnically when there was no other ground for conviction. Fourth, the Jewish leaders are represented as certainly seeking to put Jesus to death, but no other charge entailing the death penalty, no matter how inflicted, seems as relevant.

We should hold that in this, as in other regards, the Mishnah, as is generally agreed,[38] did not set forth the legal system of the Sanhedrin as it was before A.D. 70 but as an ideal. Certainly, the Sanhedrin was not at that time a council of scholars as represented in the Mishnah but was composed of an amalgam of hereditary members and scholars, as it appears in the Gospels and Josephus.[39]

My point in the last paragraph should be clarified. What I would not accept is that, in representing the legal system as an ideal, the rules in the Mishnah had no contact with reality as it existed before A.D. 70. That is, while we cannot always accept the rules in the Mishnah at face value for the period before the destruction of the Temple, we cannot discount them simply as intellectual fantasy. It is inconceivable to me that scholars, to no apparent purpose, would debate at enormous length legal and religious rules that they themselves had fabricated and that had no place in reality. For example, if the Mishnah sets out various forms of capital punishment, describes the crimes for which each is appropriate, and postulates the requirements for each separate offense, then it stretches my credulity to suggest there is no basis for this. In any event, law is a discipline that in general is slow to develop and slow to change. As a basic proposition we can say that the law of today rests not only on the law of yesterday but on that of hundreds of years ago. To some extent an analogy may be drawn from the *Digest* of the emperor Justinian. This was published in 533 as law for the Byzantine Empire and is composed of juristic texts from the Roman empire, and almost none of the texts is from a work later than 235. Of course the Byzantines were careful in what they selected, and of course modern scholars dispute the extent to which the extant texts were changed, but still it would be agreed that in the main the texts give the substance of law as it was three hundred years before. So, I suggest, it is with the Mishnah. Much may be idealized of law and of the Sanhedrin as it was before A.D. 70, but much of the actuality remains.[40]

Indeed, there is evidence from Jewish writings in Greek that in the first centuries B.C. and A.D. blasphemy was wider than uttering or cursing the name of God and that βλασφημία and βλασφημέω were the appropriate terms.

> 1 Maccabees 2.6. He saw the blasphemies (βλασφημίας) being committed in Judah and Jerusalem.

1 Maccabees was originally in Hebrew, but it has survived only in Greek and Latin manuscripts and probably was written shortly after the death of John Hyrcanus in 104 B.C.[41] The verse, as the following

verses show, concerns the defilement of the Temple by Antiochus IV. More than that, the verse says, "He saw [εἶδεν] the blasphemies" and a verb of seeing would not be appropriate for an offense that consisted solely of speech.[42]

If we can accept that the trial of Jesus was on the charge of blasphemy, then conviction at his first hearing in Mark followed on the admission that he was the Messiah. The only evidence we know of that was adduced for any crime was that he had said he would tear down the Temple and rebuild it in three days, and we know of an earlier suspicion of blasphemy when he said, "Your sins are forgiven."[43]

If it is plausible to hold that the crime charged against Jesus was blasphemy, then we should stress that the evidence adduced against him was this: "We heard him saying, 'I will throw down this temple made with hands, and within three days I will build another not made with hands'" (Mark 14.58). If such words spoken by Jesus amounted to blasphemy, then so would any claim by Stephen that Jesus would destroy the Temple.[44]

3

⁘

THE ESSENES, QUMRAN, AND THE CHARGES AGAINST STEPHEN

⁘ ⁘ ⁘

THIS CHAPTER IS IN THE NATURE OF A HISTORICAL SKETCH. I believe I have no need for the purposes of this book to discuss and decide whether the scrolls of Qumran belong to the Essenes or to some other group nor whether John the Baptist was an Essene. My limited purpose in this chapter is simply to indicate that when the early Christians diverged from mainstream Jewish religious groups such as the Pharisees and Sadducees, they might at the same time bear resemblances to, as well as show differences from, smaller Jewish groups. These resemblances and differences could play a role in the accusations against Stephen. Heretical groups were by no means unknown. The Jerusalem Talmud claims that there were twenty-four heretical sects at the time the Temple was destroyed.[1] My approach will be first to consider resemblances and differences between the early Christians and Essenes as described by Josephus and Philo. I will subsequently do the same for Christians and the people of Qumran in the light of the latter's scrolls.

Josephus described the Essenes in *War* 2.119ff. and *Antiquities* 18.18ff. From him we learn that the Essenes held their property in common (*War* 2.122, 2.127; *Antiquities* 18.20) just as did the early Christians as evidenced in Acts 2.44f. and 4.32–5.11 but for no time thereafter. Philo also stressed that they avoided private property (*Hypothetica* 11.4). They appointed stewards to take care of their common affairs (*War* 2.123), to receive their incomes (*Antiquities* 18.22), and no doubt to make distributions as necessary (*War* 2.125) just as the apostles appointed Stephen to be one of the seven in charge of distribution (6.3ff.). Philo, too, records that the Essenes gave up their income to the one appointed as steward who distributed according to need (*Hypothetica* 11.10, 11.13). Like the early Christians (2.42, 2.46f.) the Essenes prayed together and ate together (*War* 2.128f; Philo *Hypothetica* 11.11f.). Jesus opposed the swearing of oaths (Matthew 5.34ff.) as did St. James (5.12); so did the Essenes (*War* 2.135). But both the early Christians and the Essenes (*War* 2.139ff.) allowed an oath in particular circumstances. Like the Pharisees and the early Christians, but unlike the Sadducees, the Essenes also believed in the immortality of the soul (*War* 2.154; *Antiquities* 18.18). But unlike Jesus they were sticklers for purity (*War* 2.137ff., 148ff.) and observed the prohibitions on working on the Sabbath even more than other Jews (*War* 2.147ff.). Thus, in this regard, though their interpretations might differ from other Jews, they strenuously sought to follow the law of Moses. From Josephus' accounts it emerges that the Essenes were esteemed by other Jews because of their piety. The same appears from Philo.[2]

The Dead Sea Scrolls associated with the community at Qumran also indicate that property should be held communally.[3] To lie about one's property was a serious offense: "If one of them has lied deliberately in matters of property, he shall be excluded from the pure meal of the Congregation for one year and shall do penance with respect to one quarter of his food."[4] The offense is similar to that of the Christians Ananias and Sapphira in Acts 5.1ff., although their fate was more severe.[5] As with the early Christians, the communal meal and communal prayer were important: "They shall eat in common and bless in common and deliberate in common."[6]

The community also eagerly awaited the Messiah. The standard view was that there would be two Messiahs: one would dominate religious matters, and the other would rule over temporal and political matters.[7] With the messianic coming would appear "the End of Days." Since one of the Messiahs was to rule over temporal matters, "the End of Days" did not mean the end of the world but the end of the current era.

The community, as we can judge from the Damascus Covenant (CD), took very seriously the prohibition against working on the Sabbath. Thus, it reads from 10.15:

No man shall work on the sixth day from the moment when the sun's orb is distant by its own fullness from the gate (wherein it sinks); for this is what He said, *Observe the Sabbath day to keep it holy* (Deut. 5.12). No man shall speak any vain or idle word on the Sabbath day. He shall make no loan to his companion. He shall make no decision in matters of money and gain. He shall say nothing about work or labour to be done on the morrow.

No man shall walk abroad to do business on the Sabbath. He shall not walk more than one thousand cubits beyond his town.[8]

No man shall eat on the Sabbath day except that which is already prepared. He shall eat nothing lying in the fields. He shall not drink except in the camp. 11. If he is on a journey and goes down to bathe, he shall drink where he stands, but he shall not draw water into a vessel. He shall send out no stranger on his business on the Sabbath day.

No man shall wear soiled garments, or garments brought to the store, unless they have been washed with water or rubbed with incense.

No man shall willingly mingle [with others] on the Sabbath.

No man shall walk more than two thousand cubits after a beast to pasture it outside his town. He shall not raise his hand to strike it with his fist. If it is stubborn he shall not take it out of his house.

No man shall take anything out of the house or bring any-thing in. And if he is in a booth, let him neither take anything out nor bring anything in. He shall not open a sealed vessel on the Sabbath.

No man shall carry perfumes on himself whilst going and coming on the Sabbath. He shall lift neither sand nor dust in his dwellings. No man minding a child shall carry it whilst going and coming on the Sabbath.

No man shall chide his manservant or maidservant or labourer on the Sabbath.

No man shall assist a beast to give birth on the Sabbath day. And if it should fall into a cistern or pit, he shall not lift it out on the Sabbath.

No man shall spend the Sabbath in a place near to Gentiles on the Sabbath.

No man shall profane the Sabbath for the sake of riches or gain on the Sabbath day. But should any man fall into water or fire, let him be pulled out with the aid of a ladder or rope or [some such] utensil.

No man on the Sabbath shall offer anything on the altar except the Sabbath burnt-offering; for it is written thus: *Except your Sabbath offerings* (Lev. 23.38).[9]

This observance is in marked contrast to Jesus' lack of concern for obeying the prohibition against Sabbath working.

The community is famous for the strictness of its rules on ritual impurity. Above all, as is shown in more than one document, they sought to follow the law of Moses. Thus, the *Damascus Covenant* (4QDa/e) 1ff.: "And whoever has despised these rules which follow all the precepts found in the Law of Moses shall not be counted with all the sons of His truth, for his soul has rejected the just instruc-tions. As a rebel, he shall be dismissed from the congregation."[10]

It appears that the Qumran sect left Jerusalem for the desert because they regarded the Temple priests as illegitimate and found the priestly rituals no longer acceptable. This was most likely not because they were hostile to the Temple. On the contrary, they wanted to return to a purified Temple.[11] One of the most important scrolls—it is also the longest—is the Temple Scroll, which sets out in detail the rules that relate to the Temple.[12]

The early Christians, as one group among Judaism, would not appear utterly strange to the mainstream of believing and observing Jews, the Sadducees and Pharisees. They would notice the same tendency of the Christians to exclusivity and conversion of others to their beliefs, property held in common (to whatever extent), common meals and prayer, and a yearning for the coming of the Messiah.

What would be utterly strange and anathema to Sadducees, Pharisees, Essenes, and the Qumran community alike was the alleged behavior of Stephen. To them all it would be horrifying that he wished the Messiah to destroy the Temple and to change the law of Moses.

It should be emphasized that we have no evidence that other early Christians expected Jesus to destroy the Temple, or that if they did they preached it abroad.[13] Nor does it appear that they stressed that Jesus would change the Mosaic law.[14]

4

✛

THE MEANING

OF

STEPHEN'S

DEFENSE

✛ ✛ ✛

STEPHEN WAS BEFORE THE SANHEDRIN, AND THE HIGH PRIEST
asked him, "Are these things so?" (7.1).

Stephen's reply was entirely political and revolutionary, but it
has often been misunderstood or misstated and regarded as irrelevant. The classic statement of its supposed irrelevance is by Martin
Dibelius:

> The irrelevance of most of this speech has for long been the real
> problem of exegesis. It is, indeed, impossible to find a connec-
> tion between the account of the history of Israel to the time of
> Moses (7.2–19) and the accusation against Stephen: nor is any
> accusation against the Jews, which would furnish the historical
> foundation for the attack at the end of the speech, found at all
> in this section. Even in that section of the speech which deals
> with Moses, the speaker does not defend himself; nor does he
> make any positive countercharge against his enemies, for the
> words οἱ δ εοὐ συνῆκαν in 7.25 do not constitute such an at-
> tack any more than does the report of the gainsaying of Moses
> by a Jew in 7.27. It is not until 7.35 that we sense any polemic

interest. From 7.2–34 the point of the speech is not obvious at all; we are simply given an account of the history of Israel. It is not until 7.35 that the purpose becomes evident, and then we read: this Moses whom the Israelites rejected (7.35), whom they did not obey (7.39), was sent to them by God as a leader, a deliverer out of Egypt, as a prophet, as bearer of the λόγια ζῶντα (7.35–43). This change from historical review to controversy becomes quite clear from 7.35 onwards (cf. τοῦτον twice, οὗτος three times). A further tendency is seen in the section 7.44–50: God's house among the Israelites at first took the form of a tent, then the Temple of Solomon, but God does not dwell in what men have made. After this, and only in the concluding words (7.51–53), are we told the real accusation against the people: You have always opposed the revelation of God, both through the prophets and through the law! We might say that the two sections already dealt with (7.35–43 and 44–50) paved the way for this accusation. We should then have to reckon the significance of these two sections to consist, respectively, in the themes of resistance to the lawgiver Moses, and a mistaken conception of the house of God, although the latter of these two themes is only hinted at. Then we could connect them with the twofold charge against Stephen (concerning the holy place, and the customs delivered by Moses). With reference to the Temple, however, the speech is extremely reticent and seems to be very loosely connected with the charge—indeed, we ourselves shall probably be reading into it any significance that we may find. All this cannot alter the fact that the major part of the speech (7.2–34) shows no purpose whatever, but contains a unique, compressed reproduction of the story of the patriarchs and Moses.[1]

Haenchen states, "Stephen's speech offers three main difficulties about which the experts have cudgelled their brains. Let us dwell on the first before embarking on the others: Stephen is supposed to be answering the question whether he is guilty of the charge, but a very large part of his speech has no bearing on this at all."[2] Wikenhauser claims it is no real defense speech but a clever disagreement with Jewry.[3]

I find the speech wholly relevant.[4] Nor in my view is it the case that up to verse 42 "Stephen has been on common ground with his hearers,"[5] nor is this a salvation-history of Israel.[6] For clarity I will in this chapter set out the main themes in the speech. In chapters 5, 6, 7, and 8 I will set out the arguments for my understanding of the speech.

The speech may be divided into three interlinked parts. The first part has three distinct thrusts. The first thrust is on Jewishness, establishing Stephen's own, with Abraham, as the first Jew, who received the covenant from God with circumcision as the sign of the covenant (7.8). But a covenant is a contract, and the Jews must keep their part. This they (i.e., the unconverted Jews) have failed to do, and they are "uncircumcised in heart and ears" (7.51). They are not true Jews.

The second thrust of the first part is on exile and slavery. (i) God promised the land to Abraham and his descendants but did not give Abraham any of it (7.5).[7] (ii) These descendants would be resident aliens and would be enslaved (7.6). (iii) Joseph was sold into slavery in Egypt (7.9). (iv) The Jews were enslaved in Egypt (7.19). (v) Moses (7.20ff.) never reached the promised land. This is not stated in the speech, but it was too well known to need to be.

The third thrust of the first part is on the Jews' failure to follow the leader designated by God. (i) Joseph was sold by his brothers into Egypt because of their jealousy of him (7.9). The ground of the jealousy is not stated and did not need to be because it was well known to the auditors, but it was the result of Joseph saying they would bow down before him (Genesis 37.5ff.). The brothers are not termed "brothers" but are called "the patriarchs" (7.9). This is to indicate that they were the fathers of the twelve tribes, and the tribes were scattered. Thus, it brings us back to the theme of exile. (ii) Moses avenged an Israelite by killing the Egyptian who wronged him (7.24). He believed that his kin would realize that God was rescuing them through him (7.25), but they did not, and Moses fled (7.29). (iii) Moses later led the people out of Egypt, and once again they failed to follow his commands (7.39).

In the second part of the speech from verse 44 onwards, Stephen claims that Solomon built the Temple, and this was contrary to law because "the Most High does not dwell in houses made by human hands" (7.48).

The third part from verse 51 returns to the first. The Jews are "uncircumcised in heart and ears" and are always opposing the Holy Spirit just as their ancestors did. The ancestors persecuted the prophets and killed those who foretold the coming of the "Righteous One" whom the present Jews now have betrayed and murdered. Though they were the ones who received the law, they did not keep it.

Jesus is not named in the speech and indeed appears only at the end, in verse 52, as the "Righteous One." Yet the whole speech is about Jesus. Jesus is the Messiah, the Righteous One, whom Stephen—like the apostles in Acts 1.6—sees as the political Messiah. As such he is the savior of the Jews. He will bring them back from exile, and he will drive out from Israel those who enslave them, the Romans. But the Jews have rejected Jesus just as they rejected Jacob, Moses, and the prophets. They have broken the law, not kept the contract of the covenant, and are in fact uncircumcised. In other words, they are not truly Jews. They are stiff-necked, always opposing the Holy Spirit; they have not repented. But without their repentance, the Messiah cannot come from heaven to fulfill "the time of restoration of all things." In accepting that Jesus was the Messiah, the early Christians believed that they were the Jews who were right.

I claimed at the outset that the speech was revolutionary. The underlying logic is that Jesus is the Messiah who will destroy the power of the Romans and return the Jews to Israel, *provided* the Jews repent. Repentance for Stephen equals accepting Jesus as the Messiah. This the unconverted Jews have not done, and hence it is those who received the law who block the restoration of all things.

Let us return to the second part, whose theme, though less pronounced, cannot be called subordinate or subsidiary. Before he bursts into a tirade at 7.51 Stephen says:

Acts 7.44. "Our ancestors had the tent of testimony in the wilderness, as God directed when he spoke to Moses, ordering him to make it according to the pattern he had seen. 45. Our ancestors in turn brought it in with Joshua when they dispossessed the nations that God drove out before our ancestors. And it was there until the time of David, 46. who found favor with God and asked that he might find a dwelling place for the house of Jacob. 47. But it was Solomon who built a house for him. 48. Yet the Most High does not dwell in houses made with human hands; as the prophet says,

> 49. 'Heaven is my throne,
> and the earth is my footstool.
> What kind of house will you build
> for me, says the Lord,
> or what is the place of my rest?
> 50. Did not my hand make all these things?'"

Stephen does not touch directly on the accusation that he said Jesus would destroy the Temple. But now he is saying that the creation of the Temple was wrong. More than that, he seems to be saying that its continuing existence is wrong. I take it that we have here in fact an indirect admission that Stephen did repeat frequently that Jesus would destroy the Temple and that Jesus would act rightly to do so. But there is still more, as the juxtaposition of these verses and the succeeding verses shows: the Jews are wicked in not repenting and in not seeking Jesus' destruction of the Temple. Given the importance of the Temple to all right-thinking Jews, especially in Jerusalem, it can be no surprise that the trial disintegrated into a riot.

With regard to the other accusation against Stephen—that he had claimed Jesus had changed the law of Moses—little can be said with confidence. The topic is approached only in the most indirect way. The Jews who had received the law and who had not accepted Jesus, Stephen claimed, had not accepted the law (7.53). That Jesus had changed the law of Moses may have been the spin put on Stephen's message by others, not what Stephen had intended. After all, in the first, the major, part of his speech Stephen insisted on the special relationship through law of the Jews with God: the covenant with Abraham, the law given to Moses. Stephen's speech is possibly weakened if he was also claiming Jesus had changed the law. Besides, such a claim would be irrelevant to the notion of a political Messiah.

It should be made express, and the issue will recur in chapters 15 and 16, that we have no evidence as to whether the emphasis on Jesus' changing the law and destroying the Temple was, according to tradition, Stephen's alone or was a basic element of early Christianity. At this stage I wish merely to observe that no argument can be drawn from Acts 21.27ff. to the effect that the emphasis was standard and caused general hostility:

> 27. When the seven days were almost completed, the Jews from Asia, who had seen him [Paul] in the temple, stirred up the whole crowd. They seized him, 28. shouting, "Fellow Israelites, help! This is the man who is teaching everyone everywhere against our people, our law, and this place; more than that, he has actually brought Greeks into the temple and has defiled this holy place." 29. For they had previously seen Trophimus the Ephesian with him in the city, and they supposed that Paul had brought him into the temple.

The accusation that Paul spoke against the people and the law—not just against the law but also against the people, which is a charge not made against Stephen—is illuminated by Paul's speech after his arrest. He emphasizes his Jewishness and his zeal for the law (22.1ff.).

> Acts 22.21. "Then he [God] said to me, 'Go, for I will send you far away to the Gentiles.'"
> 22. Up to this point they listened to him, but then they shouted, "Away with such a fellow from the earth! For he should not be allowed to live."

The crowd erupts in anger. Paul offended against the people by saying that God had sent him to the Gentiles. By the same token Paul offended against the law: if he taught that Jesus was the Messiah, then it was contrary to Jewish tradition to take this salvation to the Gentiles: messianic salvation was for Jews alone. These two verses confirm the precision of 21.28. Paul was not charged with saying that Jesus spoke against the people and the law. He was charged with speaking against the people and the law himself.

(Some clarification is perhaps advisable. At that time Judaism was a proselytizing religion: there were Gentile converts and acolytes. But in the context of 22.21 Paul is claiming that God was sending him to Gentiles who were neither converts nor acolytes. That Gentiles might seek salvation through the Messiah might be acceptable to non-Christian Jews, but only if they sought it through Judaism.)

Likewise, the accusation was that Paul spoke against the Temple, not that Jesus did. More than that, Paul acted against it: he introduced Greeks into the Temple. It was a capital offense for a Gentile to go beyond a certain point in the Temple.[8] Not a word indicates a belief that Paul claimed that Jesus would destroy the Temple. The complaints against Paul were not those leveled against Stephen.

5

✠

STEPHEN'S SPEECH I: ABRAHAM AND JOSEPH

✠ ✠ ✠

After the courteous address "Brothers and fathers, hear me,"[1] Stephen gets straight to the point:

> Acts 7.2. "Brothers and fathers, listen to me. The God of glory appeared to our ancestor Abraham when he was in Mesopotamia, before he lived in Haran, 3. and said to him, 'Leave your country and your relatives and go to the land that I will show you.' 4. Then he left the country of the Chaldeans and settled in Haran. After his father died, God had him move from there to this country in which you are now living. 5. He did not give him any of it as a heritage, not even a foot's length, but promised to give it to him as his possession and to his descendants after him, even though he had no child. 6. And God spoke in these terms, that his descendants would be resident aliens in a country belonging to others, who would enslave them and mistreat them during four hundred years. 7. 'But I will judge the nation that they serve,' said God, 'and after that they shall come out and worship me in this place.' 8. Then he gave him

the covenant of circumcision. And so Abraham became the father of Isaac and circumcised him on the eighth day; and Isaac became the father of Jacob, and Jacob of the twelve patriarchs."

Abraham is the first Jew,[2] to whom God gave the covenant with the rite of circumcision to mark it (7.8). Nils Alstrup Dahl correctly claims, "In Stephen's speech the Jewishness of Abraham is not concealed but emphatically pronounced."[3] Stephen stresses this: he wishes to emphasize his own Jewishness, that he is a righteous Jew, that he is addressing Jews who (he is going to claim) are Jews in appearance only, sham Jews (7.51), not circumcised in spirit.

Dahl is among the many who wrongly regard this part of Stephen's speech as a summary that stresses the themes that are fundamental to the whole outline of Israel's ancient history. He suggests: "In his short summary Stephen—that is, the Stephen of Luke—has left out a number of tales: Abraham in Egypt, Abraham and Lot, the battle with the kings, Hagar and Ishmael, the three men and the destruction of Sodom, and, most remarkable of all, the sacrifice of Isaac. The account is concentrated upon Abraham's migration, God's promise, the covenant of circumcision, and the birth of Isaac."[4] But the topics left out are precisely those that have no role to play in Stephen's defense. We do not have here a general history of Abraham.

"When he was in Mesopotamia" is a quotation from the Septuagint Genesis 12.7 and an indication that Luke used that version.[5] Some scholars find the details of Abraham's wanderings unnecessary. Thus, Conzelmann says, "In recalling the travels of Abraham the stopover in Haran can be skipped over (cf. Gen. 15:7; Neh. 9:7; and to a certain degree Philo Abr. 62). Luke's strong emphasis on Haran, therefore, is striking."[6] That is correct. But in Stephen's speech the detail has a precise purpose, setting the scene for what follows. God appeared to Abraham in Mesopotamia, then in Haran, then in the land in which his descendants, the present generation, are living. That is to say, God is everywhere. He is not to be confined in a house made by human hands (7.47ff.). Stephen is preparing for his attack on the role of the Temple.[7] But that is not his main point. Stephen is emphasizing that Abraham himself will have no part in the land. That will go to his descendants who, nonetheless, will be exiles resident in a country belonging to others who would enslave them, but God will judge the nation[8] that they serve (7.5ff.). Again we are given details that at first seem irrelevant but most certainly are not. The exile and slavery directly referred to occur in Egypt. But there is a subtext in the context of Stephen's speech. Many Jews, he is saying, are in exile in foreign lands. Those who remain are under the domination of the Roman conquerors: the Israelites are thus in exile, in a land that is not theirs, even when it is the land given them by God.

This subtext of Roman domination is always present and must not be overlooked. One of the most striking features of the speech and, indeed, of the whole Stephen affair is precisely that the Romans do not appear. How can that be? They would be profoundly aware of anyone making political messianic claims even about another. They would be concerned about anything that was likely to cause a disturbance. They would keep a watchful eye on the Sanhedrin. Yet they do not seem to take any interest even after the lynching of Stephen. An explanation is offered in chapter 16.

We are faced with a dilemma in Stephen's speech. Either we say, with others, that Stephen on trial made a speech that was largely irrelevant—what could past exile and slavery in Egypt have to do with his case?[9]—or there was a coded message, here about the Romans. The dilemma appears both with regard to Abraham's wanderings and the enslavement of the Jews in Egypt—irrelevant or highly relevant politically. To me the latter seems much more plausible. But then there arises the question whether the silence about the Romans was always a feature of the speech or whether reference to the Romans was excised by Luke because it was politically uncomfortable? The precise answer has little importance in the present context, but I prefer the first alternative. Express reference to God punishing the Romans would always have been dangerous and would have been unnecessary since Stephen would know that the Sanhedrin would understand.

On this approach Stephen is making another important point. He puts words into God's mouth: "and after that they shall come out and worship me in this place" (7.7). Stephen is predicting that after the Romans have been defeated, the Jewish exiles will return to Israel and truly worship God. The political Messiah theme continues. A detail calls out for attention. This part of Stephen's speech depends heavily on the account of Abraham in Septuagint Genesis. But Stephen's speech has an important change. Septuagint Genesis 15.14 has God saying: "And the nation whomsoever they shall serve I will judge; and after this, they shall come forth with much baggage." The Septuagint's "returning with booty" has come to be for Stephen the exiles' "return worshipping God." The change has to be important. Stephen is making the point that the Jews, free from the Romans' rule, will truly worship God. For him and his defense the acquisition of booty is irrelevant.

We still have not finished with the relevance of Abraham for Stephen's defense. God's covenant with Abraham is, as a covenant, a bilateral contract[10] with obligations on both sides. Of course, the contract is unilaterally imposed by God, the Jews not being able to state terms.[11] Still, the Jews have to carry out their end of the bargain, and Stephen will claim rather later on that they have not (7.51ff.). Moreover, the covenant with circumcision as its sign was given before the law was given through Moses. The law was not there from the beginning of time nor even from the beginning of Judaism. There was, it may be understood, no need to see the law as everlasting and unchangeable. It is perhaps not too fanciful to consider that Stephen was hinting that the Messiah would have power to alter the law presented by Moses. After all, he does make Moses, the great transmitter of the law, say: "God will raise up a prophet for you from your own people as he raised me up" (7.37). Indeed, there seems to be a reference here to Deuteronomy 18.18ff.:

> "'I will raise up for them a prophet like you from among their own people; I will put my words in the mouth of the prophet, who shall speak to them everything that I command. 19. Anyone who does not heed the words that the prophet shall speak in my name, I myself will hold accountable. 20. But any prophet who speaks in the name of other gods, or who presumes to speak in my name a word that I have not commanded the prophet to speak—that prophet shall die.' 21. You may say to yourself,

'How can we recognize a word that the Lord has not spoken?'
22. If a prophet speaks in the name of the Lord but the thing
does not take place or prove true, it is a word that the Lord has
not spoken. The prophet has spoken it presumptuously; do not
be frightened by it."

The clear meaning of the Deuteronomic passage is that this prophet
will have power to change the law. And for Stephen, the prophet
that Moses is describing is Jesus.

Richard J. Dillon claims, "Stephen's argument may be divided
as follows: (1) God's way with Abraham, vv. 2–8; (2) God's way
with Joseph, vv. 9–16; (3) God's way with Moses, vv. 17–43; (4) God's
dwelling with his unfaithful people, vv. 44–50; (5) Conclusion: Israel's perennial resistance to the holy spirit and its messengers."[12]
But we have just seen that the first theme is emphatically not God's
way with Abraham; otherwise, God's demand that Isaac be sacri-
ficed would have been stressed. Now we will see that the second
theme is equally emphatically not God's way with Joseph:

> Acts 7.9. "The patriarchs, jealous of Joseph, sold him into
> Egypt; but God was with him, 10. and rescued him from all his
> afflictions, and enabled him to win favor and to show wisdom
> when he stood before Pharaoh, king of Egypt, who appointed
> him ruler over Egypt and over all his household. 11. Now there
> came a famine throughout Egypt and Canaan, and great suffer-
> ing, and our ancestors could find no food. 12. But when Jacob
> heard that there was grain in Egypt, he sent our ancestors there
> on their first visit. 13. On the second visit Joseph made himself
> known to his brothers, and Joseph's family became known to
> Pharaoh. 14. Then Joseph sent and invited his father Jacob and
> all his relatives to come to him, seventy-five in all; 15. so Jacob
> went down to Egypt. He himself died there as well as our an-
> cestors, 16. and their bodies were brought back to Shechem and
> laid in the tomb that Abraham had bought for a sum of silver
> from the sons of Hamor in Shechem."

At 7.8 we were told Jacob was the father of the twelve patriarchs.
Their status as the patriarchs is again brought up in 7.9. Stephen

emphasizes that they are the ancestors of the twelve tribes, to stress once more the theme of exile. Nothing is said about the patriarchs being Joseph's brothers nor that the reason for their jealousy was his dreams that they would bow down before him (Genesis 37.5ff.). For this there was no need, since the members of the Sanhedrin would be well aware of these facts. But implicit in the speech is that Jews failed to follow a leader—Joseph, later Moses—chosen by God to save them. We will be reminded soon (7.11ff.) that, despite everything, the leader, Joseph, did save them. In this connection Stephen calls the patriarchs "our fathers." As he did with Abraham (7.2), Stephen is linking himself and his listeners with earlier outstanding figures, this time in the context of tribulations connected with the rejection of God's appointed leader.

So remote is Stephen from discussing in these verses "God's way with Joseph" that he does not mention the central event of the attempted seduction by Potiphar's wife or Joseph's subsequent imprisonment (Genesis 39.1ff.). That is irrelevant to Stephen's case. Conzelmann correctly states: "Joseph is often understood as a type of the innocent. But it is precisely the sufferings of Joseph that are all but ignored."[13] What Stephen does instead is emphasize Joseph's success in Egypt: Pharaoh appointed him ruler over Egypt and over all his household (7.10). This foreshadows a theme that will fully emerge in Stephen's treatment of Moses: Joseph and Moses favor their kin despite the demerits of the kin, not because of any personal ill treatment Joseph and Moses have received from those in command of them. If we continue to believe that the details of Stephen's speech are relevant to his defense, then his implicit argument is that Jesus, too, acted to save the Jews despite their demerits and though he had no personal cause for animosity against the Romans. In none of the four Gospels is there the slightest indication that Jesus felt any personal hostility to the Romans. Moreover, as a Galilean he was not subject to Roman domination or to the hated Roman tax.

A comment by Roloff is incidentally instructive. He finds Luke's aim in this part of the speech to be unclear, but he states that Joseph seems to be the prototype of the diaspora Jew.[14] I would agree, though the depiction of Joseph is also much more complex.

A detail in vv. 12 and 13 is significant. Jacob sent "our ancestors" to Egypt "on their first visit." "On the second visit Joseph made himself known to his brothers." On the first visit they did not recognize Joseph. Recognition came only on the second visit. To be understood is that Jesus, the Messiah, also went unrecognized on his first visit. But the Messiah is to descend again from heaven.[15]

Stephen's account of the burial of Jacob is, as is well known, garbled.[16] According to Genesis 33.19, Jacob bought from the sons of Hamor, who was Shechem's father, a plot of land outside the city of Shechem. At the time of the Exodus, Moses took the bones of Joseph in accordance with his dying command (Exodus 13.19) and buried them at Shechem (Joshua 24.32). In the Old Testament nothing is said about the other Israelites being buried at Shechem. Genesis 50.13 says that Jacob was buried not at Shechem but in the cave of Machpelah at Hebron, which Abraham had bought as a burial site. According to Stephen (7.16) Abraham had bought a tomb at Shechem. Josephus agrees that the bodies of the Israelites were removed from Egypt, but he has them reburied at Hebron.[17] Whatever the cause of the confusion, Stephen's point is obvious (provided we regard the details of his speech as relevant): he is still stressing the theme of exile. Even those who died in exile are brought back.

Stephen's themes involving Abraham and Joseph continue when he turns to Moses.

6

✛

STEPHEN'S SPEECH II: MOSES

✛ ✛ ✛

> Acts 7.17. "But as the time drew near for the fulfillment of the promise that God had made to Abraham, our people in Egypt increased and multiplied 18. until another king who had not known Joseph ruled over Egypt. 19. He dealt craftily with our race and forced our ancestors to abandon their infants so that they would die. 20. At this time Moses was born, and he was beautiful before God. For three months he was brought up in his father's house; 21. and when he was abandoned, Pharaoh's daughter adopted him and brought him up as her own son. 22. So Moses was instructed in all the wisdom of the Egyptians and was powerful in his words and deeds."

Moses was spared the fate reserved for the male Israelite children.[1] He was saved, Stephen says, by Pharaoh's daughter and brought up as her son (7.21), an account much like that of Exodus 2.10.[2] Thus, Moses had no personal grievance against the leading Egyptians.

That Moses acquired the wisdom of the Egyptians and was powerful in words and deeds has no counterpart in Exodus but is found in both Philo and Josephus.[3] Significantly for my argument, Stephen makes no mention, as Josephus does, of the Egyptians' hostility to Moses. Stephen's point in the detail is still the same: Moses had no personal quarrel with the oppressors of the nation. Jesus and the Romans are still at the forefront of Stephen's mind. Indeed, there are several indications in the speech that Jesus is the new Moses.[4]

Stephen's account of Moses continues:

Acts 7.23. "When he was forty years old, it came into his heart to visit his relatives, the Israelites. 24. When he saw one of them being wronged, he defended the oppressed man and avenged him by striking down the Egyptian. 25. He supposed that his kinsfolk would understand that God through him was rescuing them, but they did not understand. 26. The next day he came to some of them as they were quarreling and tried to reconcile them, saying, 'Men, you are brothers; why do you wrong each other?' 27. But the man who was wronging his neighbor pushed Moses aside, saying, 'Who made you a ruler and a judge over us? 28. Do you want to kill me as you killed the Egyptian yesterday?' 29. When he heard this, Moses fled and became a resident alien in the land of Midian. There he became the father of two sons."

The theme already seen with Joseph continues: Moses acts to save a fellow-Israelite (7.24). This was apparently done openly, since Moses expected that his people would realize God was rescuing them through him (7.25). In contrast, Exodus 2.12 has Moses acting in secret: "He looked this way and that, and seeing no one he killed the Egyptian and hid him in the sand." The change in the evangelist Luke is significant whether or not he was the originator of it. Stephen is making the point that Moses gave the people the chance to recognize that God had appointed him their savior. Similarly, the implication is, Jesus made it plain to the present generation by his miracles, teaching, and resurrection that God had appointed him their savior. But the Jews refused to accept the authority of Moses (7.27f.) just as, Stephen implies, their descendants rejected Jesus. It should be noted that though Stephen uses the episode to generalize the refusal to accept the authority of Moses, nonetheless the tradition in Exodus and even that followed by Stephen was about the rejection by one man. In the Greek at verse 25 οἱ δὲ is adversative, 'But.' It is a very strong *"But* they did not understand."[5]

> Acts 7.30. "Now when forty years had passed, an angel appeared to him in the wilderness of Mount Sinai, in the flame of a burning bush. 31. When Moses saw it, he was amazed at the sight; and as he approached to look, there came the voice of the Lord: 32. 'I am the God of your ancestors, the God of Abraham, Isaac, and Jacob.' Moses began to tremble and did not dare to look. 33. Then the Lord said to him, 'Take off the sandals from your feet, for the place where you are standing is holy ground. 34. I have surely seen the mistreatment of my people who are in Egypt and have heard their groaning, and I have come down to rescue them. Come now, I will send you to Egypt.'"

Stephen returns to the theme of God's special relationship with the Jews: he is the God of Abraham, Isaac, and Jacob (7.32)—and, by obvious implication for Stephen, of the present generation. Again, God is appointing someone, Moses, to save his people (7.34), though he has previously been rejected by Jews. Again, Stephen is implying that Jesus will return as savior, despite his rejection.

Some dramatic happening was needed to produce the catharsis in Moses, namely, the burning bramble bush[6] and the voice of God (7.30). Commentators appear to be troubled and (possibly in consequence) attach little significance to the happening for the speech.[7] The problem is that there seems to be too much detail. Munck correctly observes, "In the history of Moses, Stephen went into more detail."[8] Why, after all, are we informed that God told Moses to take the sandals off from his feet. David J. Williams links this with the ground being holy; later, he says, priests would do the same in the Temple in their daily service.[9] Certainly, but why is the fact relevant to Stephen's defense speech?

The answer for me again lies in Stephen's view of the nature of Jesus. For Stephen, Moses is much more important for Jesus than are Abraham or Joseph. Stephen reports (7.37): "This is the Moses who said to the Israelites, 'God will raise up a prophet for you from your own people as he raised me up.'" The scriptural authority for Stephen, which would be meaningful to his audience, is Deuteronomy 18.15: "The Lord your God will raise up for you a prophet like me from among your own people: you shall heed such a prophet." God announces in the same chapter at verse 19: "Anyone who does not heed the words that the prophet shall speak in my name, I myself will hold accountable." For Stephen, Jesus is like Moses. The cathartic experience of the burning bush has a parallel in the cathartic experience of Jesus' baptism by John.[10] Both Moses and Jesus were known to be special before, but the experience introduces their true mission: God tells Moses he will send him to Egypt because God has come to rescue the Israelites (for Stephen, 7.34); John declares Jesus will baptize with the Holy Spirit (Matthew 3.11; Mark 1.7; Luke 3.16; John 1.33). In both these experiences that foretell rescue, God appears and speaks, but only of Jesus does he declare, "This is my Son, the Beloved with whom I am well pleased" (Matthew 3.17; Mark 1.11; Luke 3.22).[11] Thus, Jesus is greater than Moses.

The burning bush that is not consumed is, of course, a symbol. Philo's interpretation, which was presumably current, is persuasive: "The burning bramble bush was a symbol of those who suffered wrong, as the flaming fire of those who committed it."[12] The bramble bush was the Jews, and the powerful fire was the Egyptians who, however, did not prevail over them. The symbolism meant the safety of Israel despite tribulations. Baptism was the ritual sign of repentance,[13] certainly in Luke 3.7ff. It is thus also a symbol of safety brought through God, but a safety not free from care.

Still, something more is going on. Jesus made use of the episode of the burning bush as evidence of resurrection when he was debating with the Sadducees (Mark 12.24ff.).[14]

> Mark 12.26. "And as for the dead being raised, have you not read in the book of Moses, in the story about the bush, how God said to him, 'I am the God of Abraham, the God of Isaac, and the God of Jacob'? 27. He is God not of the dead, but of the living; you are quite wrong."[15]

The argument is that God said to Moses long after the days of the patriarchs that he was the God of Abraham, of Isaac, and of Joseph.

Jesus also claims that God is the God of the living, not of the dead. The conclusion is that Abraham, Isaac, and Joseph will return.[16] So Stephen's treatment of Moses has this further significance.

(Incidentally, the text provides what is perhaps the strongest evidence for Mark's connection with rabbinic tradition. What is translated as "in the story about the bush" (ἐπὶ τοῦ βάτου) is "at the bush." "The Bush" is the rabbinic term for the relevant portion of the scroll of Moses.)[17]

But, still, why does Stephen trouble to mention that God told Moses to take off his sandals? The answer lies somewhere in the recollection of the prominence of removing sandals that we find in Mark 1.7, John 1.27, and Luke 3.16: John the Baptist declares he is not worthy to untie the thong of Jesus' sandal.[18] The connection is the unworthiness of Moses before God and of John before the Messiah, and perhaps it should not be further pressed.[19]

The final two stages of Stephen's treatment of Moses are pivotal for the whole speech (7.35ff.):

> "It was this Moses whom they rejected when they said, 'Who made you a ruler and a judge?' and whom God now sent as both ruler and liberator through the angel who appeared to him in the bush. 36. He led them out, having performed wonders and signs in Egypt, at the Red Sea, and in the wilderness for forty years. 37. This is the Moses who said to the Israelites, 'God will raise up a prophet for you from your own people as he raised me up.' 38. He is the one who was in the congregation in the wilderness with the angel who spoke to him at Mount Sinai, and with our ancestors; and he received living oracles to give to us."

Stephen here makes four statements about Moses.[20] First, Moses was rejected by the Israelites as their ruler and judge, but God returned him to Egypt as their leader (7.35). Second, Moses led the Israelites out of Egypt, having performed wonderful signs (7.36). Third, Moses prophesied God would send a prophet like himself (7.37). This, I believe, turns out to be vital for Stephen's speech. Fourth, Moses was the one who in the wilderness was given living oracles to give to the people (7.38), that is to say, the law.[21] All this is to lead up to the enormity of the Israelites' next behavior:

Acts 7.39. "Our ancestors were unwilling to obey him; instead, they pushed him aside, and in their hearts they turned back to Egypt, 40. saying to Aaron, 'Make gods for us who will lead the way for us; and for this Moses who led us out from the land of Egypt, we do not know what has happened to him.' 41. At that time they made a calf, offered a sacrifice to the idol, and reveled in the works of their hands. 42. But God turned away from them and handed them over to worship the host of heaven, as it is written in the book of the prophets:

> 'Did you offer to me slain victims
>> and sacrifices
> forty years in the wilderness,
>> O house of Israel?
> 43. No; you took along the tent
>> of Moloch,
> and the star of your god Rephan,
> the images that you made
>> to worship;
> so I will remove you beyond
>> Babylon.'"

Despite all that Moses had done, emphasized again from verse 35 to 38, the Israelites still rejected Moses. Worse still, in their hearts they turned back to Egypt (7.39), thus rejecting salvation. Even worse, they made idols (7.41f.), rejecting God. For their ingratitude God forsook the Jews. The quotation in 7.42f. is almost word for word from Septuagint Amos 5.25ff., though to accord with historical events Stephen has changed the Damascus of Amos to Babylon. C. S. C. Williams reasonably asks whether Stephen uses "Babylon" because that had become a Christian term for Rome.[22]

Amos 5.25: "Have you offered to me victims and sacrifices, O house of Israel, forty years in the wilderness? 26. You took up the tabernacle of Moloch, and the star of your god Rephan, the images of them which you made for yourselves. 27. And I will carry you away beyond Damascus," says the Lord, the Almighty God is his name.

Stephen's meaning with regard to Jesus is crystal clear. Despite all that Jesus did, the present generation of Jews—signaled as those in the Sanhedrin—rejected him. They thus rejected salvation. They rejected God, who now has forsaken the Jews and will thrust them into still deeper exile. Accordingly, the Messiah will not descend from heaven.

We must return to verse 37: "This is the Moses who said to the Israelites, 'God will raise up a prophet for you from your own people as he raised me up.'" Jesus is, of course, for Stephen the prophet foretold by Moses and who will be like Moses. But Moses was more honored as a lawgiver than as a prophet, and Moses as lawgiver is deafeningly not mentioned by Stephen. Why? The silence must be explained in light of the fact that one of the two charges against Stephen was that he claimed Jesus would change the customs of Moses. I see in verse 37 a tacit admission of that charge and a repetition of the claim: for Stephen, Moses prophesized that Jesus would be like himself and thus would have authority to change the law.

7

✜

STEPHEN'S
SPEECH III:
THE JEWS'
DISOBEDIENCE
TO GOD

✜ ✜ ✜

ACTS 7.42F. MARKS A TURNING POINT IN STEPHEN'S SPEECH.
It is intimately connected with the description of Moses' career, but
it is not part of it. It represents God's reaction to the Israelites' response to Moses and God. It serves as a bridge to the passage where
Stephen most nearly deals explicitly with the charges against him.

> Acts 7.44. "Our ancestors had the tent of testimony in the
> wilderness, as God directed when he spoke to Moses, ordering
> him to make it according to the pattern he had seen. 45. Our
> ancestors in turn brought it in with Joshua when they dispos-
> sessed the nations that God drove out before our ancestors.
> And it was there until the time of David, 46. who found favor
> with God and asked that he might find a dwelling place for the
> house of Jacob. 47. But it was Solomon who built a house for
> him. 48. Yet the Most High does not dwell in houses made
> with human hands; as the prophet says,

49. 'Heaven is my throne,
> and the earth is my footstool.
> What kind of house will you build
>> for me, says the Lord,
> or what is the place of my rest?
50. Did not my hand make all these things?'"

Here we do have again a continuation of Moses' life. The Israelites had the "tent of witness"—this is the Septuagint Exodus 27.21
translation of the Hebrew "tent of meeting." This was made according to God's directions to Moses, who had seen the pattern.[1] This
time Stephen is emphasizing that the Israelites were following
God's commands. But David, who found favor with God, asked that
he might find a dwelling place (σκήνωμα) for the house of Jacob
(7.46). But, δέ—and the Greek δέ is adversative—it was Solomon
who built a house (οἶκος) for God (7.47). Stephen is drawing a distinction between Moses' tent and Solomon's Temple. It was wrong,
according to Stephen, to build a house for God, who does not live
in houses made with human hands (7.47), and he quotes Isaiah 66.1
as authority (7.49f.). "Made with human hands" hints at idolatry.[2]
A particular subtlety in the speech should not be overlooked: David,
who is cited with approval, wished a dwelling place "for the house
of Jacob." Solomon built a temple for God. But David's dwelling
place was in fact to house God—at least in the sense in which the
Temple housed God—which Stephen artfully conceals. Stephen's
subtlety here would anger the hearers for its apparent perversity.
We have a progression: Moses' "tent," David's "dwelling place,"
Solomon's "house." But the word that I—with others—have translated as "dwelling place" is etymologically derived from *tent* (σκηνή)
and could be so translated. And in the relevant Septuagint text, 2
Kings 6.5, God speaks of David wishing to build him a house. Stephen is representing David as virtuous and Solomon as the villain.
(Although I write as if Stephen spoke a speech as we have it, I am, as
usual, concerned with the tradition as we have it in Luke.)

Thus, Stephen is claiming that the existence of the Temple is a
wrong toward God and that in the context of a defense against the

charge that he had frequently asserted that Jesus would destroy the Temple.[3] The claim can only be seen as an indirect admission that the accusation is true. The logic is this: "You accuse me of saying that Jesus will destroy the Temple. The Temple is a wrong against God. Jesus as Messiah will destroy it. And that is the right thing to do!" Not only is there an implied admission, but in effect Stephen is repeating his offense and, at that, not only in public but before the Sanhedrin.

This part of the speech can only have been very offensive to the judges not just because it showed Stephen as defiant, not just because they and the great majority of Jews—including most likely the Essenes—regarded the Temple as the holy of holies, but also because it was based on an unaccepted understanding of David and Solomon. Thus, God commanded Moses at Exodus 25.8: "And have them make me a sanctuary, so that I may dwell among them." The sanctuary was nothing other than the tent of meeting. According to Scripture, therefore, God would reside in a tent that was made by human hands. A tent, but not a fixed house, was appropriate for a people on the move in the desert. But many Jews ceased to be nomads. David came to be uneasy that he himself lived in a house of cedar while the ark of God was in a tent (2 Samuel 7.2). The prophet Nathan told him to do as his mind dictated (2 Samuel 7.3). Then the word of God came to Nathan:

> 2 Samuel 7.5. "Go and tell my servant David: 'Thus says the Lord: Are you the one to build me a house to live in? 6. I have not lived in a house since the day I brought up the people of Israel from Egypt to this day, but I have been moving about in a tent and a tabernacle. 7. Wherever I have moved about among all the people of Israel, did I ever speak a word with any of the tribal leaders of Israel, whom I commanded to shepherd my people Israel, saying,—"Why have you not built me a house of cedar?"'"

God is denying David his wish, but neither in the passage quoted nor in what follows is God made to appear hostile to the idea of living in a house built by human hands. Indeed, quite the contrary:

7.12. "When your days are fulfilled and you lie down with your ancestors, I will raise up your offspring after you, who shall come forth from your body, and I will establish his kingdom. 13. He shall build a house for my name, and I will establish the throne of his kingdom forever."

So God desired a house built by human hands, not by David but by a descendant.[4] Solomon built it with the full approval of God for him to live with the children of Israel:[5]

1 Kings 6.11. Now the word of the Lord came to Solomon, 12. "Concerning this house that you are building, if you will walk in my statutes, obey my ordinances, and keep all my commandments by walking in them, then I will establish my promise with you, which I made to your father, David. 13. I will dwell among the children of Israel, and will not forsake my people Israel."

So, the present part of Stephen's speech is disingenuous or worse.[6] The offense of Solomon for him was to have God living in a house built by human hands. But according to Exodus 25.8, God wanted to live in a sanctuary built by men, a point passed over in silence by Stephen, who speaks only of the "tent of testimony" ordered by God (7.44) and does not refer to its purpose. To account for Stephen's attitude[7] I can only conclude that, from Jesus' cleansing of the Temple, coupled with the stories that Jesus would destroy the Temple, Stephen believed Jesus would in fact destroy the Temple. For Stephen, the Temple therefore had to have been constructed against the will of God.[8]

Stephen now becomes outrageous and passes to invective.[9]

Acts 7.5.1. "You stiff-necked people, uncircumcised in heart and ears, you are forever opposing the Holy Spirit, just as your ancestors used to do. 52. Which of the prophets did your ancestors not persecute? They killed those who foretold the coming of the Righteous One, and now you have become his betrayers and murderers. 53. You are the ones that received the law as ordained by angels, and yet you have not kept it."

Now he is not just discussing the behavior of past generations but addressing the members of the Sanhedrin directly about their own conduct. They are "uncircumcised in heart and ears." The words are a reminiscense of Jeremiah 9.25:

> "The days are surely coming," says the Lord, "when I will attend to all those who are circumcised only in the foreskin: 26. Egypt, Judah, Edom, the Ammonites, Moab, and all those with shaven temples who live in the desert. For all these nations are uncircumcised, and all the house of Israel is uncircumcised in heart."

Physical circumcision is not enough. Faithless Jews are not different from others who practice circumcision but who are truly uncircumcised to God. Circumcision in heart is needed, and the present generation is uncircumcised in heart.[10] They are not God's people, not true Jews. They oppose the Holy Spirit just as their ancestors did.

Their ancestors, Stephen insists, killed the prophets who foretold the coming of the "Righteous One" (the Messiah), and now the present generation has betrayed and even murdered the Messiah (7.52). In fact, it should be noted that there is no evidence to support Stephen's claim that all of the prophets were persecuted, although some were.[11]

He maintains implicitly that his own conduct has been righteous. In fact it is his judges—who have not yet judged him—who received the law of God but have not kept it (7.53). He aggressively attacks.

Stephen concludes by accusing the members of the Sanhedrin, and through them other Jews, of not following the law. This is the worst possible accusation that can be made against Jews.[12] They are "a stiff-necked people," a reference to Exodus:

> 33.2. "I will send an angel before you, and I will drive out the Canaanites, the Amorites, the Hittites, the Perizzites, the Hivites, and the Jebusites. 3. Go up to a land flowing with milk and honey; but I will not go up among you, or I would consume you on the way, for you are a stiff-necked people."

33.5. For the Lord had said to Moses, "Say to the Israelites, 'You are a stiff-necked people; if for a single moment I should go up among you, I would consume you.'"

Thus, if God were to come among the present generation of Israelites, he would destroy them. The unconverted Jews have not repented. Without repentance the Messiah cannot descend from heaven. The Jews who do not accept Jesus[13] are blocking "the time of restitution of all things" (3.21), including release from Roman domination.

It can be no surprise that the court was in an uproar (7.54).

8

+

STEPHEN'S

DEATH

+ + +

AT ACTS 7.53 WE HAD STEPHEN DECLARING THAT THE PRESENT generation of Jews had not kept the law. For the Messiah to come, the Jews had to believe that Jesus was the Messiah and that he would destroy the wicked Temple.

> Acts 7.54. When they heard these things, they became enraged and ground their teeth at Stephen. 55. But filled with the Holy Spirit, he gazed into heaven and saw the glory of God and Jesus standing at the right hand of God. 56. "Look," he said, "I see the heavens opened and the Son of Man standing at the right hand of God!" 57. But they covered their ears, and with a loud shout all rushed together against him.

The Sanhedrin was enraged—understandably so[1]—and Stephen made things worse. He had been charged with blasphemy, had in effect admitted that he had said (at least some of) the things he was accused of, attacked the judges and the present generation of Jews (and their ancestors) as breakers of God's law, and was now uttering a further wrong. He was claiming that Jesus, who would destroy the Temple and change the laws of Moses, stood at the right of God. The members of the court covered their ears to avoid hearing it (7.57), and the court broke up in uproar.[2]

Acts 7.58. Then they dragged him out of the city and began to stone him; and the witnesses laid their coats at the feet of a young man named Saul. 59. While they were stoning Stephen, he prayed, "Lord Jesus, receive my spirit." 60. Then he knelt down and cried out in a loud voice, "Lord, do not hold this sin against them." When he had said this, he died.

Thus, they lynched Stephen. I believe that the Sanhedrin had the power to put Jews to death by stoning for blasphemy,[3] but the death of Stephen is no real argument for that. The court had not given a formal verdict; a verdict of guilty that carried the death penalty required a subsequent meeting with a verdict the following morning.[4] That execution for blasphemy was by stoning and that Stephen was stoned are also no real evidence for a judicial execution for blasphemy because stoning was a common form of lynching.[5]

Still, Stephen's death does seem to contain some remnants of judicial execution. First, they dragged Stephen out of the city, as was laid down for execution by stoning in Numbers 15.35f.:

Then the Lord said to Moses, "The man shall be put to death; all the congregation shall stone him outside the camp." 36. The whole congregation brought him outside the camp and stoned him to death, just as the Lord had commanded Moses.

The practice continued. Thus, Mishnah Sanhedrin 6.1 begins: "When sentence [of stoning] has been passed they take him forth to stone him. The place of stoning was outside [far away from] the court, as it is written, *Bring forth him that hath cursed without the camp.*"[6] Still, even a lynching might be carried out outside of a city to avoid pollution.

They stoned Stephen and, we are told, "the witnesses laid their clothes at the feet of a young man named Saul."[7] It is the witnesses, not others, who removed garments in order to stone Stephen.[8] The role of the witnesses in the execution by stoning is set out in Deuteronomy 17.6f.:

On the evidence of two or three witnesses the death sentence shall be executed; a person must not be put to death on the evidence of only one witness. 7. The hands of the witnesses shall be the first raised against the person to execute the death penalty, and afterward the hands of all the people. So you shall purge the evil from your midst.

Subsequent modifications, to avoid mutilation of the body, were introduced (between 100 B.C. and 100 A.D.)[9] by the Pharisees, who believed in bodily resurrection and reasoned that mutilation could hinder resurrection.[10]

Mishnah Sanhedrin 6.4. The place of stoning was twice the height of a man. One of the witnesses knocked him down on his loins. If he turned over on his heart the witness turned him over again on his loins. If he straightway died that sufficed; but if not, the second [witness] took the stone and dropped it on his heart. If he straightway died, that sufficed; but if not, he was stoned by all Israel, for it is written, *The hand of the witnesses shall be first upon him to put him to death and afterward the hand of all the people.*[11] All that have been stoned must be hanged. So R. Eliezer. But the Sages say: None is hanged save the blasphemer and the idolater.

There is no reason to believe that this precise procedure was followed in the case of Stephen.

The Sanhedrin acted illegally, but there is much to be claimed in mitigation. The charges against Stephen, that he prophesied and wanted the destruction of the Temple and the alteration of God's law given to Moses, were the most serious that right-thinking Jews could imagine. Stephen did not deny the charges. In effect he reiterated what he was accused of: the Temple was wicked. He took the initiative and attacked the judges. It was they who broke God's law. He insisted that they were uncircumcised in truth, not true Jews. Those who did not accept Jesus prevented the coming of the Messiah and thus the expulsion of the Romans. In Stephen's view, the members of the Sanhedrin were traitors to God.

Though we have no direct evidence, we may perhaps assume that Stephen's views were not unique to him but were held by some other Christians. Otherwise it is hard to explain his prominence in Acts. But how common these views were is unclear. This is an issue that keeps cropping up.

At Acts 8.1 we read: "And Saul approved of their killing him." The statement suggests that Saul was not previously a persecutor of the Christians. It is Stephen's defense that determined Saul's attitude toward the Christians and presumably the attitude not just of Saul.

9

⊹

JESUS
AND THE
TEMPLE

⊹ ⊹ ⊹

I HAVE ARGUED THAT THE CHARGE AGAINST STEPHEN THAT he claimed with approval that Jesus would destroy the Temple was plausible and that, in fact, the charge was accurate. Now I want to discuss Jesus' attitude toward the Temple, for which I believe we have strong evidence both direct and indirect.

The direct evidence is in the so-called cleansing of the Temple.

> John 2.14ff. In the temple (ἱερόν) he found people selling cattle, sheep, and doves, and the money changers seated at their tables. 15. Making a whip of cords, he drove all of them out of the temple, both the sheep and the cattle. He also poured out the coins of the money changers and overturned their tables. 16. He told those who were selling the doves, "Take these things out of here! Stop making my Father's house a marketplace!"

The heinousness of Jesus' behavior toward Pharisees, Sadducees, and other observing Jews was brought out in my chapter 2. Jesus obstructed the payment of the Temple tax and the necessary Passover sacrifices, and he created a public disturbance and assault in the Temple precincts.[1]

The direct evidence may not show that Jesus was hostile to the very existence of the Temple, only that he was hostile to some Temple practices. Yet the obstruction of these practices, especially of providing sacrificial animals, hindered necessary religious rites.

The meaning of this direct evidence becomes clearer when we consider the indirect evidence, which lies in the relationship between Jesus and Isaiah. For me, Jesus was in the tradition of Israelite prophets, especially Isaiah.[2] Like Jesus, Isaiah stresses the corruption of Israel, the neglect of God, and the people's hypocrisy.[3] Isaiah declares that God does not want animal sacrifice;[4] perhaps a similar opinion influenced Jesus' cleansing of the Temple.[5] Indeed, Isaiah makes God condemn all sacrifices to him, even of grain and frankincense (Isaiah 66.3):

"Whoever slaughters an ox is like
 one who kills a human being;
whoever sacrifices a lamb, like
 one who breaks a dog's neck;
whoever presents a grain offering,
 like one who offers swine's blood;
whoever makes a memorial offering of
 frankincense, like one who blesses an idol.
These have chosen their own ways,
and in their abominations they take delight."

This is in the context of declaring the Temple unnecessary, perhaps even as wicked (Isaiah 66.1f.):

Thus says the Lord:
"Heaven is my throne
and the earth is my footstool;
what is the house that you would
 build for me,
 and what is my resting place?
All these things my hand has made,
 and so all these things are mine,
   says the Lord."

These verses are those quoted by Stephen at Acts 7.49f., and they are to be seen as directly relevant to the charge against him. The first part of Stephen's claim is that the Temple is contrary to God and that he has Isaiah's authority to say so. The second part of his claim must be an admission that he had said that Jesus had declared he would destroy the Temple. The third part would be that Jesus would be justified in doing so. The justification would not be because Jesus had Isaiah's authority: of that he had no need. Isaiah simply provides evidence for the correctness of Jesus' attitude.

Jesus' apparent prophecy that the Temple would be destroyed seems to be a deliberate reference to the arrogance of the Israelites in Isaiah 9.8ff.:

> The Lord sent a word against Jacob,
>> and it fell on Israel;
> 9. and all the people knew it —
>> Ephraim and the inhabitants of Samaria —
> but in pride and arrogance of
>> heart they said:
> 10. "The bricks have fallen,
>> but we will build with dressed stones;
> the sycamores have been cut down,
>> but we will put cedars in their place."

The emphasis on the "dressed stones" is repeated in Mark 13.1ff., with "'Look, teacher, what large stones and what large buildings!' Then Jesus asked him, 'Do you see these great buildings? Not one stone will be left here upon another; all will be thrown down.'"[6] In Isaiah the implication is that the dressed stones will fall, just as the bricks fell. The prophesy in Isaiah is about the destruction of a replacement building that will be constructed. Jesus' prophesy is about the destruction of the second Temple, also a replacement building—the first Temple was destroyed in 63 B.C.—that was under construction.

Isaiah objected to the observance of the Sabbath and festivals.[7] Time and again Jesus appeared to be a Sabbath breaker. Like Jesus (Matthew 12.10ff.; Mark 6.52, 7.14ff., 8.14ff.) Isaiah favored incomprehension by the people. God said: "Go and say to this people: 'Keep listening, but do not comprehend; keep looking, but do not understand'" (Isaiah 6.9).[8] Like Jesus (Mark 5.25ff.), Isaiah's God was not troubled by female uncleanliness: he is depicted as a woman giving birth (Isaiah 42.14) and as a midwife (Isaiah 66.9) (who becomes unclean by contact).

Seen against the background of Isaiah, Jesus' behavior in cleansing the Temple becomes comprehensible. His behavior shows, first of all, that he was hostile to animal sacrifice. More than that, it demonstrates that he was hostile to the payment of the Temple tax by anyone.[9] But to be hostile to the payment of the Temple tax is inevitably to be hostile to the Temple. It is thus very reasonable to hold that Jesus thought the Temple should be destroyed. If he believed he was the Messiah, then he believed he should, and would, destroy it.

(A crucial difference between Isaiah and Jesus should be noticed: Isaiah spoke, but Jesus acted. Isaiah opposed animal sacrifice in theory, but Jesus obstructed it in the here and now, at Passover. Zechariah 14.21 also expresses a desire that trading in the Temple should stop, but at the same time the writer is emphatically in favor of animal sacrifice.)

The main argument against my conclusion would be drawn from the "den of robbers" quotation in the Synoptics, to indicate that his anger was really against corruption, but any such argument would be weak:

> Mark 11.17. He was teaching and saying, "Is it not written, 'My house shall be called a house of prayer for all the nations'? But you have made it a den of robbers."

Matthew 21.13 and Luke 19.46 have no equivalent to "for all the nations." (A much weaker version is in John 2.16.) But there is no evidence that the sellers of the sacrificial animals charged exorbitant prices or that the money changers exorbitant rates. Indeed, such behavior seems unlikely given the control exercised by the priests. Moreover, the "den of robbers" notion in Mark 11.17 makes no sense when set against Mark 11.15: Jesus drove out not only the sellers but their supposedly innocent victims, the buyers.[10] Again, Mark 11.18 has as a reaction to Jesus' behavior the priests' desire to kill him; this would be an exaggerated response if he had acted only to inhibit an abuse. The quotation in Mark is a composite from Isaiah 56.7 and Jeremiah 7.11. Isaiah contains the idea of a house of prayer for all peoples but nothing about a den of robbers. Jeremiah asks if God's house has become a den of robbers in the sight of the Israelites, but their crimes were committed outside.

In my view the quotation in Mark is a later insertion into the tradition because of a failure to understand Jesus' behavior. In any event, the quotation does not correspond to Stephen's understanding, which is our real concern.[11]

In conclusion, I should like to suggest that, if Jesus' cleansing of the Temple was motivated by Isaiah, we may have an explanation for the Jewish leaders' hesitation to arrest Jesus for fear of the crowd and for Pontius Pilate's reluctance to execute him. They suspected many understood his stance.

10

✠

ENCODEMENT

✠   ✠   ✠

Stephen's speech is, as I have suggested, partially in code. Encodement is a well-known mode of passing information to those with the wit to understand while hiding the message from those not so alert. Perhaps the prime home of coded message is in declarations of romantic passion and in illicit assignations. In Boccaccio's *Decameron* the noblewoman who wants a lover sends coded messages to him who understands through a priest who does not.[1] Still, encodement is found in many contexts. It is used by adults in front of children whom they do not want to enlighten.[2] It is frequent in Dutch seventeenth-century genre paintings.[3] Notoriously it is present in modern advertising where pretty women are in effect represented as the gain to be derived from drinking a particular alcoholic beverage or driving a specific car. John Hale writes of princely authority in the Renaissance: "What could not be said directly, as an order from ruler to subject, was diffused allegorically in paintings and entertainments designed for small audiences but to be widely talked about."[4] Alison Lurie has noted that successful books written for children contain coded messages of opposition to adults.[5] It is even found in some biblical laws or perhaps even in all biblical laws ascribed to Moses.[6]

Two standard settings for coded messages are more particularly relevant for us: fables where animals talk and parables. In both, the message is deeply encoded. I am, of course, not suggesting that

Stephen's speech is a fable or a parable. But a basic point of fables is that they contain a message from the weak about the strong. And Stephen is in a weak position. Jesus' parables to a great extent contained his message, and they would be a part of Stephen's everyday life.

Prime among fables where animals talk are the fables of Aesop and the Uncle Remus tales of Joel Chandler Harris (1840–1908). One of the features of these fables is the intention to pass on indirectly a message from the weak that would be unpalatable to the strong if stated bluntly. The animal speaks but with the mind of the slave. The animal can say things that the slave cannot.[7] It is not surprising that Aesop is said to have been a slave[8] and that the ex-slave Uncle Remus may be shown as loving the little white boy but sometimes nonetheless as passing on revolutionary messages in disguise. A constant theme is the weak getting the better of the strong by the use of guile.[9] Even when the strong seems to prevail, the tables can still be turned. Thus, Brer Fox caught Brer Rabbit with his Tar-Baby, and his victory seemed assured, even at the end of the story.[10] But subsequently, Brer Fox gloried in his triumph:

"'Well, I speck I got you dis time, Brer Rabbit,' sezee; 'maybe I ain't, but I speck I is. You been runnin' roun' here sassin' after me a mighty long time, but I speck you done come ter de een' er de row. You bin cuttin' up yo' capers en bouncin' roun' in dis naberhood ontwel you cum ter b'leeve yo'se'f de boss er de whole gange. En den youer allers some'rs what you got no bizness,' sez Brer Fox, sezee. 'Who ax you fer ter come en strike up a 'quaintence wid dish yer Tar-Baby? En who stuck you up dar whar you iz? Nobody in de roun' worril. You des tuck en jam yo'se'f on dat Tar-Baby widout waitin' fer enny invite,' sez Brer Fox, sezee, 'en dar you is, en dar you'll stay twell I fixes up a bresh-pile and fires her up, kaze I'm gwineter bobbycue you dis day, sho,' sez Brer Fox, sezee.

"Den Brer Rabbit talk mighty 'umble.

"'I don't keer w'at you do wid me, Brer Fox,' sezee, 'so you don't fling me in dat brier-patch. Roas' me, Brer Fox,' sezee, 'but don't fling me in dat brier-patch,' sezee."

Brer Rabbit's uppityness had got him into this trouble. He would welcome any death so long as he was not thrown into the brier patch, he claimed. So Brer Fox throws him in the middle of a brier patch. Brer Rabbit "hollers out":

> "'Bred en bawn in a brier-patch, Brer Fox—bred en bawn in a brier-patch!' en wid dat he skip out des ez lively ez a cricket in de embers."[11]

The audience for the original of this fable was not the white master but the black slave. Even so, the moral of the story could not be expressed.

Harris' narrator is an integral part of the fable, and Uncle Remus obtains benefits, even expressly, from his tale: Christmas gifts from causing a pleasant surprise,[12] Christmas leavings,[13] a piece of mincemeat pie.[14] The encodement is to be regarded as successful.

The narrator does not obtrude in person in Aesop in the same way.

> A timid old man was grazing his donkey in a meadow when all of a sudden he was alarmed by the shouting of some enemy soldiers. "Run for it," he cried, "so that they can't catch us." But the donkey was in no hurry. "Tell me," said he: "if I fall into the conqueror's hands, do you think he will make me carry a double load?" "I shouldn't think so," was the old man's answer.—"Then what matter to me what master I serve as long as I only have to bear my ordinary burden?"[15]

The intended audience for this could be slave or owner. The narrator certainly reports it as a poor man's lack of interest in a change of government, but it fits better in a private context, which, indeed, is where it is sited. In fact, making it a fable about a change of government is itself part of the encodement.

The significance of Stephen's speech is plain: to some extent he has to encode his message, which is that, with the proper attitude of the Jews toward Jesus as Messiah, Jesus will throw out the Romans. Closer to home for Stephen are Jesus' parables, which can almost be seen as a direct precedent. These parables are so coded that they are often difficult to understand. Indeed, Jesus even claimed that he spoke in parables so that those who were not his disciples would not understand (Luke 8.9f.).[16] But parables are different from fables with talking animals. The latter can be taken at face value, but the former cannot. Parables force listeners to try to understand the message. The same is true of Stephen's speech. One of these parables will be enough for our purposes:

> Luke 20.9. He began to tell the people this parable: "A man planted a vineyard, and leased it to tenants, and went to another country for a long time. 10. When the season came, he sent a slave to the tenants in order that they might give him his share of the produce of the vineyard; but the tenants beat him and sent him away empty-handed. 11. Next he sent another slave; that one also they beat and insulted and sent away empty-handed. 12. And he sent still a third; this one also they wounded and threw out. 13. Then the owner of the vineyard said, 'What shall I do? I will send my beloved son; perhaps they will respect him.' 14. But when the tenants saw him, they discussed it among themselves and said, 'This is the heir; let us kill him so that the inheritance may be ours.' 15. So they threw him out of the vineyard and killed him. What then will the owner of the vineyard do to them? 16. He will come and destroy those tenants and give the vineyard to others." When they heard this, they said, "Heaven forbid!" 17. But he looked at them and said, "What then does this text mean:[17]
>
> 'The stone that the builders
>   rejected
>   has become the cornerstone'?
>
> 18. Everyone who falls on that stone will be broken to pieces; and it will crush anyone on whom it falls." 19. When the scribes and chief priests realized that he had told this parable against them, they wanted to lay hands on him at that very hour, but they feared the people.

This time Jesus' meaning was too clear. The chief priests and Pharisees (or scribes) understood his meaning with the result that they wanted to arrest him.[18]

Likewise, Stephen's speech was not so encoded as to fail to be understood by the Sanhedrin, nor, as I will argue in the next chapter, could it be intended to be. The response of the Sanhedrin to breaking the code was to lynch him. Modern commentators, further from the scene, have not broken the code.

But still in this chapter my main point is that encodement has its place in speeches in criminal trials. Two situations spring immediately to mind. First, one party wishes to play on a judge's or jury's racial or sexual prejudices, but cannot do so openly. Second, a goverment is hated, perhaps as a foreign oppressor, and the defense believes the judge may be sympathetic to illegal acts of the accused. In fact, encodement is everywhere in legal cases. One example may be the trial of Bernhard Goetz, "the subway vigilante."[19] A basic message was that a group of exuberant black youths is by its nature dangerous, and a violent response with a gun is always justified. Again, S. F. C. Milson writing of the limitations placed on dispositions of property in the seventeenth century has stated: "Although undertaken by judges, this was an essentially legislative process motivated by policy. But since courts cannot easily be explicit about such operations, individual decisions in the seventeenth century were justified by whatever line of argument lay nearest to hand."[20]

In fact, encodement is fundamental in the legal process. The whole history of English law, so largely judge-made, is inconceivable without it. Witness the use of fictions to bring an action before a particular court stating something to be the case that everyone knows is false: for instance, that the colony of Virginia was situated in the ward of Cheap in London.[21] Encodement, indeed, is often institutionalized in law. Two further precise examples, one from Rome, one from England, will suffice.

At Rome, the state did not introduce means by which owners might free slaves. But manumission developed. One standard mode was called *manumissio vindicta*. Someone who wished to free his slave would appear before the praetor (the elected official in charge of the court) with his slave. A friend of the owner would claim that the person held as a slave was free, the owner would put up no defense, and the praetor would declare the slave to be free. The true facts were obvious and probably not concealed even the first time the device was tried. The law even took account of the facts behind the encodement: thus, the former owner, who was now apparently someone who had wrongly held a free person as a slave, acquired the rights of a patron.[22]

In England, after the statute *De Donis* of 1285 gave statutory recognition to entails, land would descend without the possibility of alienation so long as heirs emerged from the prescribed class. Often heirs wished to alienate land, and lawyers came to their aid. One device, known as common recovery, appears in the fifteenth century. The tenant in tail in possession, say A, wishes to sell in fee simple to B. B brings a real action claiming the fee simple. A appears in court vouching C, a man of straw, for warranty. C does not deny his obligation to warrant A's title, but asks for an adjournment to discuss a settlement with B. When the adjournment is granted, C disappears, thus being in contempt of court, and the judge adjudges the land in fee simple to B.[23] Naturally, the true facts were known to everyone, including the judges who were hostile to perpetuities.[24]

A fine biblical example of encodement is in 2 Samuel. King David committed adultery with Bathsheba, who became pregnant. When a subterfuge to have her husband, Uriah, have sex with her failed, David arranged that Uriah would be killed in battle (2 Samuel 11.1ff.). Then:

2 Samuel 12.1. And the Lord sent Nathan to David. He came to him, and said to him, "There were two men in a certain city, the one rich and the other poor. 2. The rich man had very many flocks and herds; 3. but the poor man had nothing but one little ewe lamb, which he had bought. He brought it up, and it grew up with him and with his children; it used to eat of his meager fare, and drink from his cup, and lie in his bosom, and it was like a daughter to him. 4. Now there came a traveler to the rich man, and he was loath to take one of his own flock or herd to prepare for the wayfarer who had come to him, but he took the poor man's lamb, and prepared it for the man who had come to him." 5. Then David's anger was greatly kindled against the man. He said to Nathan, "As the Lord lives, the man who has done this deserves to die; 6. he shall restore the lamb fourfold, because he did this thing, and because he had no pity."

7. Nathan said to David, "You are the man! Thus says the Lord, the God of Israel: 'I anointed you king over Israel, and I rescued you from the hand of Saul; 8. I gave you your master's house, and your master's wives into your bosom, and gave you the house of Israel and of Judah; and if that had been too little, I would have added as much more. 9. Why have you despised the word of the Lord, to do what is evil in his sight? You have struck down Uriah the Hittite with the sword, and have taken his wife to be your wife, and have killed him with the sword of the Ammonites.'"

To get David to recognize his fault, Nathan presents him with his behavior in a parallel situation. David condemns the wrongdoer; Nathan in the name of God condemns David.

It might be suggested that I lay too much stress on encodement for an explanation of Stephen's speech[25]—but then why do scholars experience such difficulty in understanding?—and that I should look rather to an exploitation of Scripture in the form of the Septuagint. From that, the notion is, the artificiality of the Stephen episode would be apparent. This exploitation would be of the story of Naboth's vineyard,[26] which is recounted in the Septuagint at 3 Kings 20, in the Hebrew Bible at 1 Kings 21. Ahab coveted Naboth's vineyard; Naboth refused to exchange or sell. Jezebel, to please her unhappy husband-king, sent a letter to the community leaders telling them to set a feast, putting Naboth in a chief place, with the sons of two transgressors in front of him. These two were to testify against him that he cursed God and the king. The leaders did so, and consequently they took Naboth out and stoned him. The exploitation of this episode by Luke, the suggestion would be, is (1) Stephen supposedly blasphemed by speaking against God and Moses; Naboth was accused of cursing God and the king; and Moses is to be regarded as the model king; (2) in both cases the accusation is false; (3) in both cases the result was a lynching, not a judicial execution. I am not convinced of any dependence of Luke on the story of Naboth. First, the overall differences in the accounts are great. Second, the notion of false witnesses is a commonplace and is no indication of dependence of one account on another. Moreover, the emphasis in Stephen's speech on the wrongness of the Temple makes no sense if the witnesses were false. Third, in the story of Naboth there is no sign of a formal trial, which is central to Stephen, nor of a defense speech, which is the highlight of the Stephen affair.

11

✢

THE LOGIC

OF

STEPHEN'S

SPEECH

✢ ✢ ✢

In chapter 4 I set out my understanding of the meaning of Stephen's speech, and in chapters 5 through 8, the stages of the speech in order. Here, in the hope of obtaining greater clarity, I will set out the underlying logic.

1. God established Abraham as the first Jew with a covenant whose sign was circumcision (7.8). A covenant is typically bilateral.[1] The present generation of Jews are "uncircumcised in heart and ears" (7.51), they have not kept their side of the contract, and consequently they are not true Jews. *To be understood:* (a) Stephen, as a Jew, is addressing Jews. (b) They are not true Jews because they have not repented; that is, they have not accepted Jesus as the Messiah. (c) They are the guilty ones.

2. God commanded Abraham to leave Mesopotamia but did not allow him any part of the promised land (7.2ff.). The patriarchs, the founding fathers of the dispersed twelve tribes, sold Joseph into a foreign land, Egypt (7.9).[2] Moses left Egypt and "became a resident alien in the land of Midian" (7.29). Led by Moses, the Israelites wan-

dered in the desert (7.36), but Moses never set foot in the promised land. *To be understood:* (a) Exile has been the lot of the Jews. (b) The Messiah will return the dispersed Jews to the promised land, as did Abraham and Moses, and end the exile.[3] (c) The Messiah can return from heaven only when the Jews repent. (d) Jesus is the Messiah. (e) For Jews not to accept Jesus as such is to prevent the coming of the Messiah and the return of the dispersed to Israel.

3. Joseph was enslaved in Egypt (7.9), but despite the hostility of his brothers, he saved them from death (7.14ff.). Subsequently, the Jews were slaves in Egypt (7.19). Moses, despite lack of acceptance, brought the Jews out of Egypt into the promised land (7.30ff.). *To be understood:* (a) Enslavement has been the lot of the Jews. (b) The present generation of Jews are in effect in slavery, under foreign domination by the Romans. (c) Despite lack of acceptance by fellow Jews, both Joseph and Moses saved the Israelites. (d) Despite lack of acceptance by fellow Jews, Jesus intends to save the Jews, that is, free them from foreign, Roman, domination.

4. Joseph's authority over his brothers, which was determined by God, was not accepted by them (7.9). Moses' authority over the enslaved Jews, which was determined by God, was not accepted by them (7.25ff., 7.39ff.). The prophets, determined by God, were persecuted (7.52). *Expressed:* The present generation rejected, betrayed, and murdered the "Righteous One," that is, the Messiah, Jesus (7.52).

5. A further theme, precise but implicit, responds to one of the grounds of the accusation: The Temple is wicked and contrary to the wishes of God (7.47ff.). *To be understood:* (a) The Messiah will destroy the Temple. (b) The destruction of the Temple is to be wished for.

Stephen's speech fits into a well-known genre of legal defense. The emphasis in such speeches is not that the accusations are untrue. Their truth may even be admitted. The heart of the defense is really a battle for the soul of the court or even of the nation. A clear American example is the trial that began in September 1969 of the so-called Chicago Seven for conspiracy and for making speeches to "incite, organize, promote, and encourage" antiwar riots in Chicago during the Democratic National Convention in 1968.[4] The backdrop was the U.S. government's commitment to the war in Vietnam. An immediate consequence of the guilty verdict on five of the defendants was rioting on campuses throughout the nation. The immediate consequence of Stephen's trial was the first organized persecution of Christians (8.1ff.). As is common with such defenses, in both trials the defense itself grabbed the limelight.[5]

But Stephen's defense speech has a further prominent feature: it is partly encoded. Stephen is facing two enemies, and his public utterances have probably been too blatant for him to escape either. He is before the Sanhedrin charged with blasphemy. In view of the witnesses that he claimed Jesus had changed the law of Moses and would destroy the Temple, his only possible defense would involve maintaining that Jesus was the Messiah. But the Messiah, as Stephen and many others envisaged him, would drive out their conquerors, the Romans, and return the exiled Jews to Israel. Stephen's only hope—a slim one—was to persuade the Sanhedrin without exposing its members to further danger from the Romans. The coded message from Jewish history could be easily understood by fellow Jews, less easily by outsiders. Besides, being in code and hence indirect, as in the case of talking animals in fables, his speech might have appeared less offensive: he was not directly confronting his judges, at least not until verse 51 when he was presumably carried away.

Stephen might also have been conscious that Jesus frequently expressed his message by parables which, by their very nature, are in code. He might also have remembered the intervention of Gamaliel in the trial of Peter and John, which I quoted in chapter 1 from Acts 5.33ff. Gamaliel, a Pharisee who was not convinced by the claims of Peter and John about Jesus, nonetheless argued that the Sanhedrin should leave them alone. His argument—from rather garbled history which we will look at in chapter 15—was that if the claims were false, the movement would fail. But if Jesus were the Messiah, he said, the Sanhedrin would not be able to overthrow his followers and might even be fighting against God (5.39). For release Stephen might not need to persuade the judges but simply raise a reasonable doubt: Jesus could be the Messiah. But he also was on very slippery ground. The high priest was in effect appointed by the

Romans, and though technically he held office for life, in practice he held the office only so long as the Romans allowed.[6] Moreover, the priests whose office was hereditary were almost of necessity collaborators with the Romans, even against their will. Otherwise, their lives were at risk. The supposed example of Herod in Josephus *Jewish Antiquities* 14.175 is instructive. When he overcame Hyrcanus, he killed all members of the Sanhedrin.[7] At any time only those Sanhedrin members who were not overtly hostile to the government would survive as well as keep their own privileged position. So, for the advantage of his judges, Stephen had to avoid alienating the Romans further.

A further complicating factor was that, of necessity, Stephen's defense was a missionary speech. He was convinced of the rightness of his position and of the basic falsity of his judges' powerful stance. In this he may be compared with Jan Hus.[8] But in one important regard Stephen was more successful than Hus: his speech was not continually interrupted. This may have been one consequence of encodement.

A striking feature of the Stephen affair is the total absence of the Romans. But it is inconceivable that they were unaware of, or indifferent to, the public unrest and disturbance. Luke has omitted their presence either because, in the conditions of the time, it was politically unwise to notice their presence or because they were not necessary in Luke's theology. We may assume that the Romans merely watched.[9]

Stephen cannot deny the accuracy of the accusations: what he had said was too well known. His defense is justification in that what he said was true. Truth is not always an adequate defense in a criminal trial, but it could be in this case. If Jesus were the political Messiah who would destroy the Temple because it was contrary to God's wishes and alter the customs of Moses, then Stephen spoke no blasphemy. The problem for the defense—and Stephen tries to deal with it—is that Jesus has not returned as the Messiah. On this basis Stephen must establish the following facts:

A. He must first establish his Jewishness, not in the genealogical sense—that could be taken for granted—but as pious, traditional, and right-thinking. He must show, in fact, that he is not attacking Judaism. This he sets out to do from the very beginning by calling Abraham "our ancestor," and he continues in that vein.

B. He must show that he believes God has a very special relationship with the Jews and that he, Stephen, has no concern for the spiritual well-being of Gentiles. This he does by stressing God's covenant with Abraham, the contract with the Jews.

C. He must show that the Messiah he awaits is the political Messiah. To do this he stresses the need for such a Messiah: the Jews are dispersed, in exile from the land God promised them, and subject to foreign domination. He adduces example after example of Jewish dispersion, exile, slavery. Only the political Messiah will end this dispersion and slavery. In this demonstration Stephen shows the orthodoxy of his thought.

D. He must explain why it is that with the Jews' special relationship with God they nonetheless have suffered and are still suffering exile and foreign domination. His argument here is that the Jews have repeatedly broken their contract with God and are still breaking it. In particular they refuse to accept the leaders God appointed for them.

E. Specifically, he must show that it is proper for him to expect and want Jesus to destroy the Temple. His argument is that God does not dwell in a house made by human hands. The Temple is contrary to God's wishes. God had instructed Moses to make a tent in accordance with the pattern he showed him.

F. Above all, he must explain why Jesus has not returned as Messiah. Stephen's argument is the one he used about dispersion and foreign domination. Until the Jews follow God's law and repent, they will suffer. The Messiah (who is Jesus) has not come because the Jews have not repented and accepted him as the Messiah.

The matter should also be viewed from another angle. How else was Stephen to defend himself? He could not simply deny that he had claimed Jesus would destroy the Temple and change the law of Moses. That he had so claimed was surely too well known. Nor would it be a defense that he believed Jesus would so act. Nor would it be enough simply to claim that Jesus was the Messiah: to destroy the Temple and change the law were not traditional messianic attributes. The only defense was a good offense. The Jews had always fought against God and were the real lawbreakers. As such they were preventing the return of the Messiah.

Stephen's speech is a very tightly crafted defense speech. It is no rambling, irrelevant discourse on God's way with Abraham, God's way with Joseph, God's way with Moses, God's dwelling with his unfaithful people, Israel's permanent resistance to the Holy Spirit and its messengers. Its themes are Jewish exile and slavery (to be ended with the coming of the Messiah) and Israel's resistance to the wishes of God, more particularly to his messengers (especially now to the Messiah, Jesus, who cannot return until the Jews repent). An integral part is the climax. The members of the Sanhedrin were infuriated and ground their teeth at Stephen (7.54). But Stephen gazed into heaven and saw the glory of God. "'Look,' he said, 'I see the heavens opened and the Son of Man standing at the right hand of God'" (7.57). Commentators have noticed the strange detail but not its significance: Jesus is standing, not as is usual sitting, at the right of God.[10] For Stephen, the Messiah is ready, waiting to return.

12

✢

THE TRIALS
OF
JESUS AND
STEPHEN

✢ ✢ ✢

ONE OF THE MOST DEBATED ASPECTS OF THE STEPHEN affair is the nature of the traditions on which his speech is based. This will be the subject of chapters 14 and 15. Here I wish to consider only one aspect of the issue: the relationship of the trial of Jesus to that of Stephen. Richard J. Dillon's account sets the scene:

> The narrative about Stephen in 6.8–15 has its organic continuation in 7.55–8.3, with the great speech probably a secondary insertion in the middle of the story (Dibelius, *Studies*, 168). The narrative, which Luke received at least in part from his source, fluctuates in its portrayal between a judicial proceeding and a lynching, presumably because Luke augmented the source account with elements of a Sanhedrin trial in order to configure the protomartyr's death to Jesus' (Conzelmann, *Apg.*, 51; Schneider, *Apg.*, 1.433–34). The parallelism between the two "martyrdoms" is typically Lucan in that ingredients of the Synoptic passion story omitted in Luke 22–23 are brought for-

ward here for the process against Stephen (e.g., vv. 13–14 = Mark 14.57–58). The reprise of Jesus' passion in Stephen's will include the false witnesses, the high priest's question, the "Son-of-Man" vision (7.56), and the dying prayers (7.59–60; cf. Richard, *Acts*, 6.1–8.4, 281–301). At the same time, the Sanhedrin-trial setting permits Stephen's martyrdom to fall into a climactic series with the earlier persecutions in Acts, the first having ended in mere threats (4.17, 21), the second with scourging (5.40) and a resolve to kill (5.33) which will now reach fruition (Haenchen, *Acts*, 273–74).[1]

Dillon is certainly correct in centering on the Gospel account in Luke. If the same person is the author of both Luke and Acts, then any modeling of Stephen's trial on that of Jesus will relate to the account of the latter as it is found in Luke rather than in the other three Gospels. This is so whether Luke or Acts was written first. What is surely striking is rather the absence of parallelism between Luke's trial of Jesus and the trial of Stephen in Acts.

Prominent in the arrest of Jesus is the role of the betrayer Judas (Luke 22.47ff.) and the denial of Peter (Luke 22.54ff.). No such drama presages the trial of Stephen. This is not because of an absence of Christian backsliders: Ananias, with his wife, Saphira, as accomplice, had earlier held back part of the proceeds of the sale of their land from the common fund (5.1ff.). The sharing of property plays its role in the Stephen affair, but betrayal does not. Jesus was led not to the Sanhedrin but to the high priest's house, where he was mocked and beaten (Luke 22.54, 63ff.). This illegality and brutality have no parallel in the story of Stephen.

The morning following Jesus' arrest, the Sanhedrin met.

Luke 22.66. When day came, the assembly of the elders of the people, both chief priests and scribes, gathered together, and they brought him to their council. 67. They said, "If you are the Messiah, tell us." He replied, "If I tell you, you will not believe; 68. and if I question you, you will not answer. 69. But from now on the Son of Man will be seated at the right hand of the power of God." 70. All of them asked, "Are you, then, the

Son of God?" He said to them, "You say that I am." 71. Then they said, "What further testimony do we need? We have heard it ourselves from his own lips!"

This hearing of Jesus in Luke is vastly different from that of Stephen. There is no mention here as in Acts (6.13) of witnesses, false or otherwise; there is in contrast to Acts 6.13f. no mention of any claim that he would destroy the Temple. Jesus only replies, "You say that I am" (Luke 22.70), that is, the Son of God. There is nothing akin to Stephen's masterly oration that holds center stage (7.2ff.). Instead, it is the behavior of the judges, especially of the high priest, that dominates the trial of Jesus. At the beginning of his trial Stephen was transfigured (6.18), but Jesus' countenance is not mentioned.

> Luke 23.1. Then the assembly rose as a body and brought Jesus before Pilate. 2. They began to accuse him, saying, "We found this man perverting our nation, forbidding us to pay taxes to the emperor, and saying that he himself is the Messiah, a king."

The Sanhedrin did not hold the second hearing that was necessary for conviction in a case that carried the death sentence.[2] In fact, it is not clear that this assembly should be regarded as a regular criminal trial. If it were, then it is surprising that it was broken off and that Jesus was handed over to the Romans (Luke 23.1f.). Moreover, the three accusations made to Pilate were only partly religious: perverting the nation, which probably corresponds to the leading of a town to idolatry of Mishnah Sanhedrin 7.4 and which was penalized by stoning; forbidding Jews to pay taxes to the Romans, which was purely a secular offense against the Romans and which could have been of no serious interest to the Sanhedrin;[3] and claiming to be the Messiah, a king, which would be both blasphemy and sedition against the Romans. In Stephen's trial, there is no such confusion: the Sanhedrin's concern is only with a religious crime, and the Jewish authorities do not involve the Romans. Indeed, a surprising feature of the Stephen affair is the total absence of the Romans.

After all this, I do not believe that it can be sensibly maintained that Luke has remodeled the tradition of the trial of Stephen to resemble that of Jesus. No argument of artificiality in Stephen's speech can be sustained on that account.[4] Nor can it really be argued, I think, that Luke fashioned the trial of Jesus so that he could later bring in elements for the much less important trial of Stephen.

Of course, the possibility must still be considered that the tradition of Stephen's speech was altered to bring it into line with the trial of Jesus, not by Luke but by other early Christians. The only possible argument for this different attempt to parallel the two trials would be that in Matthew 26.60f. witnesses, also described as false, appeared who claimed Jesus would destroy the Temple. Any such argument would be worthless. We have already seen that such an accusation could have appeared plausible at the time of Jesus' trial. But, above all, after the destruction of the Temple by the Romans in 70 A.D., any witnesses to the effect that Jesus claimed he would destroy the Temple would have to be categorized by Christians as "false." Jesus clearly had not done so.

I conclude, therefore, that Stephen's trial was not modeled on that of Jesus.

13

⊹

THE SECOND
SPEECH OF PETER,
STEPHEN'S
SPEECH, AND
PSALM 105

⊹ ⊹ ⊹

IN THE PREVIOUS CHAPTER I ARGUED THAT THE TRADITION of the trial of Jesus, especially as set out in Luke, was remarkably different from the trial of Stephen, hence one could not plausibly argue that Stephen's speech was an artificial construction designed to create parallelism. But parallelisms do exist between the speech of Stephen and the second speech of Peter in Acts.

One day Peter and John healed in the name of Jesus Christ a man who had been lame from birth (3.1ff.). The people saw him walking and praising God, and they recognized him and were full of wonder (3.9f.). The man clung to Peter and John in Solomon's Portico, and the people rushed to watch them (3.11). Peter did not waste the opportunity to spread his message.[1]

He addressed the crowd as "Israelite men," and asked why they wondered, as if it were the piety and power of himself and John that had worked the miracle (3.12). The God of Abraham, of Isaac, of

Jacob, of "our ancestors," he claimed, glorified his servant Jesus (3.13). Thus, just as Stephen later does before the Sanhedrin (7.2ff.), so Peter claims kinship with those listening to him. They are Jews, with the same God, who was also the God of their ancestors; and like Stephen, Peter expressly refers to Abraham, Isaac, and Jacob. But there are two differences between the speeches to this point. First, unlike Stephen, Peter does not link these ancestors with the themes of exile, slavery, and the disobedience of the people: naturally enough because, although these themes are the substance of Stephen's defense, they are not central to Peter. Second, at this early stage Peter, but not Stephen, claims Jesus as the servant of God and links him with the God of their ancestors. But both Peter (3.14) and Stephen (7.52) call Jesus "the Righteous One" or "the Just One."[2]

Peter goes on to state that his hearers rejected Jesus and handed him over to Pilate and that in fact they killed him (3.13f.). God raised him from the dead, and through faith in the name of Jesus, the name itself healed the cripple. Peter continues:

> Acts 3.17. "And now, friends, I know that you acted in ignorance, as did also your rulers. 18. In this way God fulfilled what he had foretold through all the prophets, that his Messiah would suffer."

Here there is a great difference between Peter and Stephen. For both, the Jews killed Jesus. But Peter is conciliatory: the people acted through ignorance. Stephen is violently confrontational: "You stiff-necked people, uncircumcised in heart and ears" (7.51). Moreover, for Peter, the people are not really to blame: they acted as they did so that God would fulfil what he had foretold through his prophets; that is, what the people did was foreordained! Stephen allows the Jews no justification. When he mentions the prophets, it is to claim that the present generation of Jews oppose God just as their ancestors did; these ancestors persecuted all of the prophets and killed those who foretold the coming of Jesus (7.52). Confrontation continues. Again for Stephen there is no suggestion that it was necessary to God's plan that Jesus suffer.

Peter expressly calls for repentance:

Acts 3.19. "Repent therefore, and turn to God so that your sins may be wiped out, 20. so that times of refreshing may come from the presence of the Lord, and that he may send the Messiah appointed for you, that is, Jesus, 21. who must remain in heaven until the time of universal restoration that God announced long ago through his holy prophets."

Peter urgently wants the people's repentance, and this is, in effect, faith in Jesus. This repentance is necessary for the Messiah to descend from heaven to earth. And for Peter, the people's repentance seems possible. In Stephen's speech, the notion of repentance is implicitly present but to a different effect. Stephen stresses throughout the people's defiance of God and the absence of repentance. They are the ones who received the law and have not kept it (7.53). Stephen does not need to state that they will continue not to keep it. The very way he addresses them at verse 51 shows he has no expectation of their repentance. They are preventing the coming of the Messiah.

Peter concludes:

Acts 3.22. "Moses said, 'The Lord your God will raise up for you from your own people a prophet like me. You must listen to whatever he tells you. 23. And it will be that everyone who does not listen to that prophet will be utterly rooted out of the people.' 24. And all the prophets, as many as have spoken, from Samuel and those after him, also predicted these days."

Stephen makes the same claim about Moses foretelling that God would raise up a prophet from his people (7.37). But Peter makes the claim with gentle and tender effect: the prophets predicted the same, and his listeners are descended from the prophets. Only at this stage does Peter bring in God's covenant with Abraham: "In your descendants all the families of the earth shall be blessed" (3.25). Stephen also introduces God's covenant with Abraham (7.8) but to different effect. For Stephen it was the covenant of circumcision, and the present generation are "uncircumcised in heart and ears." For Peter the covenant was something blessed. For Stephen it was a contract that the Jews broke and for which they had suffered and would suffer gravely.

Thus, many of the same elements appear in the two men's speeches. But these elements are used to such different purposes that it is hard to believe that Stephen's speech was molded to achieve some parallels with Peter. A much simpler explanation is that they occur in both because they had a common core in contemporary Christian dialogue. Early Christians stressed that they were Jews, nor can this surprise if they believed Jesus was the Messiah. The stress, though, is an indication if any is needed of a tension between Christian Jews and unconverted Jews. The Christians emphasized God's special covenant with Jews and their descent from Abraham and the prophets. The prophets had a special role for them insofar as they foretold the coming of the Messiah—which was, of course, by no means the only role of the prophets. They emphasized the Messiah because for them Jesus was the Messiah and, at that, the political Messiah. Consequently, in their thinking, repentance—faith in Jesus—by other Jews was vital: without that, the Messiah would not descend from heaven.

The common elements in Peter's second speech and in Stephen's speech go back to a common core in early Christian dialogue. But that dialogue itself descended from a Jewish tradition to which the early Christians belonged. The best illustration for our purposes is Psalm 105, which has been described as "a hymnic recital of Israel's history from the ancestors to the Exodus and conquest. The presence of the patriarchs and Joseph in the historical recital (e.g., Joshua 24.2–4) is unique in the psalter."[3] In what follows I will use the version of the psalm in the Septuagint not because I think it was the model for Peter or Stephen but because this is the version Luke would most likely have known.

Give thanks to the Lord, and call upon his name; declare his works among the heathen. 2. Sing to him, yea, sing praises to him: tell forth all his wonderful works. 3. Glory in his holy name: let the heart of them that seek the Lord rejoice. 4. Seek the Lord, and be strengthened; seek his face continually. 5. Remember his wonderful works that he has done; his wonders, and the judgments of his mouth; 6. you seed of Abraham, his servants, you children of Jacob, his chosen ones.

7. He is the Lord our God; his judgments are in all the earth.
8. He has remembered his covenant for ever, the word which he commanded for a thousand generations: 9. which he established as a covenant to Abraham, and he remembered his oath to Isaac. 10. And he established it to Jacob for an ordinance, and to Israel for an everlasting covenant: 11. saying, To you [singular] will I give the land of Canaan, the line of your inheritance: 12. when they were few in number, very few, and sojourners in it. 13. And they went from nation to nation, and from one kingdom to another people. 14. He suffered no man to wrong them; and he rebuked kings for their sakes: 15. saying Touch not my anointed ones; and do my prophets no harm. 16. Moreover he called for a famine upon the land; he broke the whole support of bread.[4]

The psalm is addressed to God's chosen, the descendants of Abraham and Jacob. God's covenant was given to Abraham and his oath to Isaac, and he established it to Jacob for an ordinance and an eternal covenant to Israel. The covenant is described as if it were a unilateral promise of bounty to the Israelites, not a bilateral contract under which the Israelites had to do their share (Psalm 105.11): God promised the Israelites the land of Canaan. The psalmist makes several observations. First, God made his promise when the Israelites were few in number (Psalm 105.12). Second, the Israelites spent time in exile (Psalm 105.13). Third, God did not allow others to harm them, especially not to hurt the prophets (Psalm 105.14f.). Verse 16 is not entirely clear and seems elliptical. God caused famine in the land, but we are not told why. My understanding is that the verse is a necessary transition to introduce the story of Joseph. God's unstated reason for the famine was that his prophets had been harmed. By whom? We are not told, but it can only be the Israelites in the shape of the patriarchs. If this interpretation is correct, the verse is one of the most instructive in the whole psalm. The psalmist's main theme is God's covenant with the people of Israel, to give them the land of Canaan, to protect them from foreign harm, to punish those who hurt them. That the covenant imposed obligations on the Israelites is downplayed, as is the fact that they failed to meet these obligations:

> 17. He sent a man before them; Joseph was sold for a slave. 18. They hurt his feet with fetters; his soul passed into iron, 19. until the time that his cause came on; the word of the Lord tried him as fire. 20. The king sent and loosed him; even the prince of the people, and let him go free. 21. He made him Lord over his house, and ruler of all his substance; 22. to chastise his rulers at his pleasure, and to teach his elders wisdom.

The psalmist is continuing with this approach. Joseph was sold for a slave (Psalm 105.17), but we are not told that it was by the patriarchs. Emphasis is placed on the evils that the Egyptians inflicted on him (Psalm 105.18) until God delivered him and Pharaoh gave him authority.

> 23. Israel also came into Egypt, and Jacob sojourned in the land of Ham. 24. And he increased his people greatly, and made them stronger than their enemies. 25. And he turned their hearts to hate his people, to deal craftily with his servants. 26. He sent forth Moses his servant, and Aaron whom he had chosen.
> 27. He established among them his signs, and his wonders in the land of Ham. 28. He sent forth darkness, and made it dark; yet they rebelled against his words. 29. He turned their waters into blood, and slew their fish. 30. Their land produced frogs abundantly, in the chamber of their kings. 31. He spoke, and the dog-fly came, and lice in all their coasts. 32. He turned their rain into hail, and sent flaming fire in their land. 33. And he smote their vines and their fig trees; and broke every tree of their coast. 34. He spoke, and the locust came, and caterpillars innumerable, 35. And devoured all the grass in their land, and devoured the fruit of their ground. 36. He smote also every first-born of their land, the first fruits of all their labour. 37. And he brought them out with silver and gold; and there was not a feeble one among their tribes. 38. Egypt rejoiced at their departing: for the fear of them fell upon them.

The Israelites were ill-treated in Egypt (Psalm 105.24), but there is no emphasis in the psalm on slavery or exile. The stress is very different from the necessary emphasis in Stephen's speech. It is on the retribution of God on the people of Egypt for persecuting the Israelites. This retribution is recounted with great detail (Psalm 105.27–38). In fact, this is by far the most detailed part of the psalm. But this emphasis on God's vengeance on foreigners who oppress the Israelites is lacking in the speeches of Peter and Stephen. Stephen says nothing of the terrors inflicted on the Egyptians, only: "He (Moses) led them out, having performed wonders and signs in Egypt, at the Red Sea and in the wilderness for forty years" (7.36). The psalmist's concern is not that of Stephen. The psalm continues:

> 39. He spread out a cloud for a covering to them, and fire to give them light by night. 40. They asked, and the quail came, and he satisfied them with the bread of heaven. 41. He clove the rock, and the waters flowed; rivers ran in dry places.

The stress in the concluding portion of the psalm is on God's goodness to Israel (Psalm 105.39ff.). God remembered his covenant, and he gave bounteously as he had promised (Psalm 105.42ff.). Only at the very end, and with little emphasis, are we told the reason for God's goodness: that the Israelites might keep his ordinances and seek out his law (Psalm 105.45). But there is nothing in the psalm to remind us of Deuteronomy 11.26ff., which is so relevant to Stephen:

> "See, I am setting before you today a blessing and a curse: 27. the blessing if you obey the commandments of the Lord your God that I am commanding you today; 28. and the curse if you do not obey the commandments of the Lord your God, but turn from the way that I am commanding you today, to follow other gods that you have not known."

I have devoted considerable space to Psalm 105 because of what it reveals about the speech of Stephen. The psalm, Peter's speech, and Stephen's speech are all in the same tradition, but they have different goals. All three emphasize the history of Israel. The psalmist praises God's gifts to Israel: his covenant, presented primarily as a unilateral gift, and his retribution inflicted on the enemies of the Israelites. The Israelites' wickedness toward God is downplayed; so are prophecies, and nothing at all hints at the Messiah. Peter's speech is geared toward acceptance by the Jews of Jesus as the Messiah. It is a missionary speech. Nothing is said about God's punishment of foreigners—that is irrelevant. Repentance will bring the Messiah who was promised by God. Stephen's speech is even more pointed: the Jews' exile and slavery, their wickedness toward God and the leaders God appointed, the evil of the Temple, and the Jews' murder of the Messiah whom they hold back from redeeming them.

14

✛

SOURCE-CRITICISM

✛ ✛ ✛

SCHOLARS WILL HAVE BEEN SURPRISED, PERHAPS EVEN shocked, that to this point I have said so little about sources in Acts. After all, the question of the use Luke made of his sources for Acts is perhaps the major battleground of New Testament scholarship. I have a number of reasons.

My first reason stems from my starting point in my claim that Stephen's speech as it stands is very relevant to his defense. If I have failed to establish the plausibility of this claim, then I have simply failed in this book, and my views of the sources are unimportant.

My second reason is a corollary of this. To a large extent, scholarly views on the sources in Acts depend on the author's understanding of the events he is discussing. If he fails to understand the event, then his views of the sources must be suspect. In addition, there is a danger of circularity of argument: from the understanding of the event to the nature of the sources; from the understanding of the sources to the nature of the event.

My third reason is the combination of the first two. If Stephen's speech can be regarded as a defense, then the question of Luke's sources becomes less significant. Here I am thinking of the tradition, not at all of historical accuracy, which is a very different issue.

My fourth reason is the absence of any outside marker that would lend credence to one view of the sources against any other. For the life of Jesus we have four prime versions in the Gospels. Differences between one version and another may be weighed against one another. In the absence of an external marker, as is the case with Acts, there are no objective criteria, and arbitrariness tends to prevail.

My fifth reason is that for almost any phrase, sentence, verse, or episode, the possible claims about source material are numerous:

1. Luke had one source which he (more or less) faithfully followed.

2. Luke had a tradition which he may not have understood or faithfully reproduced.[1]

3. Luke had two or more sources which he (more or less) faithfully followed and combined.

4. Luke had sources, one or more, which he altered very freely to set out his own message.

5. Luke had no sources, and the phrase, sentence, verse, or episode was a complete fabrication for the enlightenment of his audience.

6. The phrase, etc., was not in the original version of Luke but was a later insertion of unknown date or provenance.

The problems are well brought out in Haenchen's helpful summaries of the views of others. Here is his treatment of the death of Stephen:

> Critical scholarship sensed here from an early date a conflict between lynch law and orderly trial proceedings. Source-research suggested three solutions: (a) the source spoke of an act of terrorism, but the reviser introduced a court-trial (thus, e.g., Weiss, *Einl.*, 2d ed., 1889, 574n. 5; Wendt, 134n. 2); (b) the source spoke of a regular trial, but the reviser introduced features of "popular" justice (Loisy, 308); (c) two sources were worked together, one speaking of a trial, the other of a lynching (Feine, 186f., 190ff.; Spitta, 96ff.; J. Weiss, 498f.; Jüngst, 67ff.).
>
> But these conclusions as to sources have no solid foundation. Luke did not imagine the High Council as a worthy body keeping strictly within the letter of legality, but as an assembly capable of any act of violence and carried away, unchecked, by

its passion (5.33, 23.10). Hence he could portray the behavior of the authorities as exhibiting both juridical and anarchic features.[2]

As will have been noticed from chapter 8, my understanding of what went on is much the same as that of Haenchen, and I arrived at it without any consideration of the sources. But Haenchen now takes us further and argues for a tradition behind Luke. His argument is persuasive. He argues that to this point the apostles have been center stage: the abrupt switch to Stephen can only be because of a tradition that Luke cannot ignore. Again, hitherto the main enemies of the Christians for Luke have been the Sadducees. The sudden switch to bitter enmity from the Hellenists can only be attributed to a preexisting tradition. Finally, for Haenchen, Luke's explanation of why Stephen was accused is unsatisfactory and points to a tradition. With all of this I would agree. Haenchen's thesis is, at the same time, the most plausible approach for any event when there are no contrary indications and also the simplest: Luke was not inventing but had a source that was well known in his community, which Haenchen (appropriately) does not define more closely. The more complex theses of other scholars seem to have in common a lack of understanding of what may happen with law in action: hence recourse is made to a multiplicity of sources.

Haenchen's summary of scholars' views on the makeup of Stephen's speech naturally is longer:

> [E]xegetes have sought either to show that he does really answer the charge, or to explain why he does not. Some maintain that the speech has one consistent theme related to the accusation. According to F. C. Baur (*Vorlesungen über NT Theologie*, 1864, 337) this was the antithesis between the wondrous works of God and Israel's constant ingratitude. But this is a theme— very general at that—which the listener must first discover for himself and apply to the speech; even then it does not entirely fit! Hence Spitta suggested another theme: Moses as the type of the Messiah. Yet only a few verses speak of this, and what has it to do with the concrete accusation? Accordingly Wendt (138) hit upon a third theme: the idea that God's saving pres-

ence is not limited to the Temple. Unfortunately this allegedly principal idea is nowhere actually expressed, and Wendt was driven to concede a secondary theme in the Moses-Jesus analogy. Williams, in his survey (100ff.), also reports the theses of R. P. C. Hanson and B. S. Easton, the first of whom mentions three themes, the second two. But this means that the speech has no consistent theme.

At this point there appeared two ways out of the impasse. Wendt followed one: the present text must be distinguished from the original speech. The latter "naturally" dealt with the accusation. But the "source" did not make this connection clear; the "reviser" therefore introduced instead the Moses-Jesus antithesis. On this reading, the "authenticity" of the speech goes by the board, and the "tradition-or-composition" problem looms ahead. To this W. Foerster offered the following solution in 1953: only the part concerning Moses certainly goes back to Stephen; for the rest, Luke reproduces certain ideas of Stephen's circle which he had learned from Philip the Evangelist (27). This conjecture is based on the consideration that the polemical antithesis of Moses and Jesus is germane to the charge and appropriate to a militant speech; the rest Luke accepted because historically it had to do with Stephen's movement. But that Luke for this reason only filled up so important an exposition with irrelevant material is at variance with all we know of his manner of proceeding.

The second way out is that the speech has one consistent theme, indeed, but offers no defense against the indictment! Thus Beyer (1933): Stephen "says nothing about himself or the charges against him" (49). Lake (also in 1933) seconds this: " . . . religious or political pioneers when brought to court never attempt to rebut the accusations brought against them, but use the opportunity for making a partisan address" (*Beg.*, 4:70). This is perhaps too sweeping. But even if it is not, what has the first half of the speech to do with Stephen's cause? In the upshot, Bauernfeind decided, in 1938, that "the historical right of the speech to bear the concrete name of Stephen" was "purely relative" (131). As long ago as 1913, however, Wellhausen had said the same thing in clearer terms: "The speech is . . . an erudite disquisition based on the Septuagint" (13). In the same year Preuschen—taking his cue from Overbeck, p. 94—had maintained that the author was using the demonstration of Israel's constant ingratitude to open up the way for the mission to the Gentiles (39). Loisy took the argument a stage further in 1920: the redactor is explaining to Gentile readers that God's people is not Israel, but the Christians (318ff.). Thus all these scholars see the speech no longer in terms of Stephen's historical situation (hence from the viewpoint of its *composition*).

Dibelius now donned the mantle of succession, roundly declaring: "The speech was inserted . . . by Luke in the . . . Martyrdom of Stephen which lay before him." If so, why does it not deal more strongly with the accusation? Beyer had already (49) called the speech a sermon of the kind used to interpret the history of God's people in the synagogue on feast-days. Dibelius supposes that Luke employed a text of this kind in the narrative part of the speech, but he supplied the polemical sections himself and, of course, revised the whole. "In substance"—once again there is an echo of Overbeck—"the speech prepares for the separation of the Christians from the synagogue. It is no typical martyr's speech, for neither the benefits nor the dangers of martyrdom find expression" (*Studies*, 168f.). H. W. Surkau (1938) reaches the same conclusion: the speech does not belong to the Martyrdom: it is not the speech of a martyr, but a sermon (109). Trocmé also shares this view (1957): Stephen's long speech has little connection with the turbulent scene in which it has been inserted; the survey of Israel's history belongs to the Christian kerygma (212); the Martyrdom of Stephen could not have contained such a speech (208).

There we have, spread before us, the long road travelled by criticism up to the present. From Riehm's staunch conviction that Saul noted down Stephen's words in the very courtroom (Zahn, 246, still has Paul attend the sitting as an *auscultator!*) it leads to the thesis that Luke revised for his own ends the historical survey contained in a Hellenistic synagogue sermon.[3]

I have set out the account in Haenchen at considerable length, not just to indicate economically the range of views that have been held but even more to indicate the difficulties for source-criticism when we have absolutely no outside control for possible sources.[4]

If my arguments in previous chapters are correct, we need not see any multiplicity of conflicting sources nor believe that Luke was radically altering his sources.[5] The simplest solution is again the most plausible: Luke was following an established tradition. This time we have a further positive argument for this approach unless one holds the most unlikely view that Acts was written before A.D. 70. One of the accusations against Stephen was that he claimed Jesus would destroy the Temple (6.13). And I have argued in chapter 2 that the accusation was plausible and in chapter 7 that Stephen tacitly admitted (7.47ff.) that the accusation was true. But the Temple was destroyed by the Romans in A.D. 70. Thereafter, no accusation that Jesus would destroy the Temple was plausible, and no admission by Stephen would be possible. The accusation and the speech—at least this part—go back to a tradition before A.D. 70 and hence are not a product of Luke's imagination. Further arguments will be offered in the next chapter.

15

⊹

LUKE-ACTS
AND THE
STEPHEN
AFFAIR

⊹   ⊹   ⊹

ONE PROBLEM THAT IN ALL PROBABILITY WILL NEVER BE
satisfactorily solved is whether Stephen ever actually made such a
speech at his trial. It might be possible to show that he did not, but
it would be difficult to prove that he did.

One feature of the problem is that the opening chapters of Acts
are so different in character from the later chapters and from the
Gospel of Luke. The opening chapters of Acts depict the doings of
the earliest Christians. We have no evidence otherwise of their behavior. A common view is that before Luke wrote, there was no
written source for their beliefs and actions. The early Christians are
not believed to have had much reason to transmit their beliefs and
behavior to subsequent generations. In any event, we have no outside information on their attitudes.

In the Gospel of Luke, on the other hand, the evangelist was
writing on matters where there were in all probability established
traditions in writing, notably the Gospel of Mark and Q, as well as
other versions.[1] Luke himself records that many had undertaken to

set down in writing an orderly account of what had happened, as the facts had been handed down by eyewitnesses (Luke 1.1f.). Moreover, Luke's predilections, understandings, and prejudices can to some extent be recovered because we have competing versions in Matthew, Mark, and John. It would appear that in part he was writing to correct (at least the emphasis of) Mark, his major source. No doubt, too, his approach was colored by the audience he wanted to reach.

Likewise, the later chapters of Acts have a different feel. The evangelist writes as if he were, at least at times, an eyewitness and even a participant. He was, in contrast, certainly not an eyewitness to the events that led up to Stephen's death. Still, the Gospel of Luke and later Acts may be used to throw some light on the evangelist in a way that illuminates the trial of Stephen.

Striking features of the Gospels are the tightness of structure in Mark that is weakened in Luke (and Matthew) and an understanding of Judaism in Mark that is much less evident in Luke (and Matthew).[2] Two examples of the former feature that also involve the latter will suffice.[3] One thing that must not be overlooked in Mark is the progression in the episodes involving law. The episodes tend to occur in groups, with the group introducing a new stage. In Mark 1, as it now is, there are four distinct episodes concerned with law, and they interconnect. On the Sabbath Jesus cured a man possessed of an unclean spirit (Mark 1.21ff.). This he did in public. He did it by words alone, thus without breaching the prohibition against working on the Sabbath. Immediately thereafter, so still on the Sabbath, he cured Simon's mother-in-law by a laying on of hands (Mark 1.29ff.). Thus, he breached the prohibition on Sabbath working. But this he did in private, inside a house in the presence only of his disciples. "When evening came, after sunset," people brought their sick to be cured (Mark 1.32). The repetition only in Mark—evening had come, and the sun had set—emphasizes that the Sabbath had ended. So although the people had seen him cure without working, the idea of respect for the Sabbath is depicted as so strong that people waited until it ended before they approached him. Later in the chapter he cured the leper by a laying on of hands (Mark 1.40ff.). Thus, he made himself unclean (Leviticus 13.45f.): this was unnecessary because he had already shown that his words were sufficient. This laying on of hands was in private, otherwise he would not have commanded the leper to tell no one. Still, he also told the leper to show himself to the priest and make the offerings commanded by Moses.

The episodes contrast public and private healings: in fact the order is public, private, public, private. In the private healings, Mark shows Jesus as regarding himself as beyond the law: he worked on the Sabbath, he made himself unclean. But Mark also shows Jesus as far from confrontational. In the first public healing, on a Sabbath Jesus cured without working: in the second it is emphasized that the Sabbath was over. Again, though Jesus made himself unnecessarily unclean, he ordered the cured leper to follow the law. These four legal episodes all concern a miracle, specifically of healing.[4]

The four legal episodes recur in Luke, but some of the structure is lost. At Luke 4.33ff., Jesus healed the man with the unclean spirit in public in the synagogue on the Sabbath, again without touching so again without working. At Luke 4.38ff., still on the Sabbath in private Jesus cured Simon's mother-in-law but with no mention of touching, hence without working. At Luke 4.40ff., "as the sun was setting," Jesus cured by a laying on of hands those who were brought to him: that the Sabbath had ended is mentioned only once, not stressed in Luke as it is in Mark. At Luke 5.13ff., Jesus cured a leper by touching, thus making himself unclean. This he did in private, but again telling the leper to tell no one. Thus, in Luke, the division remains public, private, public, private, but the structure is otherwise lost. First, at Luke 5.1ff. there intervenes a further specified miracle but not of healing: the unexpected catch of fish. The unity of the four episodes of Mark is gone. Second, in the third episode Mark emphasizes that the Sabbath had ended; Luke does not. Mark wishes to stress that at the beginning of his mission—not later— Jesus did not publicly work on the Sabbath. Third, in the second episode in Luke, he cured Simon's mother-in-law—so far as we can tell—without working. As a result Jesus' making himself unnecessarily unclean by touching the leper but telling him to tell no one stands by itself and is inexplicable. In Luke, the retention of public, private, public, private is without purpose. For Mark, it was to show that Jesus at this stage was essentially nonconfrontational, though he had no regard for the prohibition against working on the Sabbath or for ritual purity.

The second example to show that Luke has a weaker structure than Mark with regard to rabbinical law is Peter's denial of Jesus after Jesus' arrest. David Daube has observed that a Jew, questioned by a Gentile, must not deny his Jewishness even at the risk of his life. Daube points out that the rabbis made two basic distinctions: first between evasion and a direct no; second between a private and a public denial.[5] This is precisely the pattern that is found in Mark 14.66ff. Peter was warming himself in the courtyard when a servant girl of the high priest saw him and said, "You also were with Jesus of Nazareth" (Mark 14.67). Peter responded, "I neither know nor understand what you are saying" (Mark 14.68). This reply was a denial in private and an evasion. Peter went outside to the forecourt. The maid saw him again and said to bystanders, "This man is one of them" (Mark 14.69). Peter made the same denial,[6] so again he evaded the question, but this time he did so in public. Subsequently, the bystanders said that he was surely one of them (Mark 14.70). Peter began to curse and swear, "I do not know the man of whom you speak" (Mark 14.71). This was a direct no, and it was made in public. Daube hesitates to claim that Mark is historically accurate. So would I, and I would rather feel that Mark has here a deliberate reminiscence of the rabbinic structure with a possible purpose. That possible purpose is to indicate to Christians how they should act if challenged by unbelievers.[7]

Peter's three denials of Jesus are also found in Matthew, Luke, and John, so they clearly were very much part of the tradition. It is reasonable to believe that Matthew and Luke depend to some extent on their most important source, Mark.

Luke, with whom we are concerned, shows no understanding of the rabbinic categories. A maid saw Peter as he sat by the fire among others (Luke 22.55f.). She said, "And this man was with him" (Luke 22.56). She spoke of Peter in the third person, so she was not addressing him as "you" but was speaking to the others. Peter replied, "I do not know him, woman" (Luke 22.57). So Peter's first denial is a direct no and is public. A little later, another said: "You are one of them" (Luke 22.58). We are not told that Peter had moved from the fire where others were. Peter replied, "Man, I am not" (Luke 22.58). So Peter's denial was again a direct no and presumably was public. About an hour later another said, "In truth this man was also with him, for he is a Galilean" (Luke 22.59). We are still not told Peter had moved from the fire. Peter said, "I don't know what you are saying" (Luke 22.60). Thus, in Luke, Peter's first two denials are direct and the third is an evasion; the first certainly in public, the second and third presumably so.[8]

More immediately to our purpose, however, are those passages that directly show a lack of sensitivity on the part of the evangelist to Judaism or Jewish history. In Mark 12.13–37 after the cleansing of the Temple, there is the celebrated episode of the four questions, which has been so convincingly handled by David Daube.[9] Daube observes that they correspond to the rabbis' classification of questions into four types: (1) Questions of wisdom, about law: "Is it lawful to pay taxes to the Romans?" (2) Questions of vulgarity: "Will the dead need sprinkling on resurrection because they have been in contact with a corpse?" (3) Questions of the proper way of the land: "Which is the first commandment?" (4) Questions of interpretation, on apparent contradictions: "How can the scribes say the Messiah is the son of David?" The four questions appear in a section of the Passover *haggadah*, the traditional Passover Eve service.[10]

In Luke 20.21–44 there are only three questions.[11] The structure is broken. The other question, about piety, appears in a different context in Luke 10.25ff. The connection with Jewish ritual is lost. We have a further concern with the last question, whose point has caused enormous controversy, though its immediate aim is to claim that the Messiah is not descended from David. Mark (12.35ff.) recounts this version:

> While Jesus was teaching in the temple, he said, "How can the scribes say that the Messiah is the son of David? 36. David himself, by the Holy Spirit, declared,
> > 'The Lord said to my Lord,
> > "Sit at my right hand,
> > until I put your enemies under
> > > your feet."'

37. David himself calls him Lord; so how can he be his son?"
And the large crowd was listening to him with delight.

Compare this with Luke 20.41ff.:

> Then he said to them, "How can they say that the Messiah
> is David's son? 42. For David himself says in the Book of
> Psalms,
> > ' The Lord said to my Lord,
> > " Sit at my right hand,
> > 43. until I make your enemies your
> > > footstool."'
> 44. David thus calls him Lord; so how can he be his son?"

The Markan version has a significant detail that is missing from
Luke: "And the large crowd heard him gladly" (Mark 12.37). Why
does the crowd listen to Jesus with delight in Mark when nothing is
said to that effect in Luke (nor in Matthew 22.42ff.)? I have argued
elsewhere [12] that in Mark Jesus is hinting very strongly that he is the
Messiah, and for that he must explain that the Messiah need not be
descended from David. Of the Synoptics, only Mark does not give
a genealogy of Jesus, whereas Matthew 22.41ff. and Luke 3.23ff.
spell out his descent from David. At that, illogically for them, he is
descended through Joseph! The crowd wants the Messiah to come;
they have wondered about Jesus. Now in Mark they are delighted,
for the obstacle of Jesus' birth is removed. Mark has a precise point;
Luke and Matthew have not.

This lack of comprehension of Jesus' argument by Luke the evangelist becomes even more important for this book when we look at
the same writer's argument, attributed to Peter, that is in Acts.
Peter has just claimed that the Israelites, according to God's plan,
had killed Jesus by the hands of those outside the law. Then:

> Acts 2.24. "But God raised him up, having freed him from
> death, because it was impossible for him to be held in its power.
> 25. For David says concerning him,
> > 'I saw the Lord always before me,
> > for he is at my right hand so
> > > that I will not be shaken;

26. therefore my heart was glad, and
>   my tongue rejoiced;
>   moreover my flesh will live
>   in hope.
27. For you will not abandon my soul
>   to Hades,
>   or let your Holy One experience
>   corruption.
28. You have made known to me the
>   ways of life;
>   you will make me full of gladness
>   with your presence.'

29. Fellow Israelites, I may say to you confidently of our ancestor David that he both died and was buried, and his tomb is with us to this day. 30. Since he was a prophet, he knew that God had sworn with an oath to him that he would put one of his descendants on his throne. 31. Foreseeing this, David spoke of the resurrection of the Messiah, saying, 'He was not abandoned to Hades, nor did his flesh experience corruption.' 32. This Jesus God raised up, and of that all of us are witnesses. 33. Being therefore exalted at the right hand of God, and having received from the Father the promise of the Holy Spirit, he has poured out this that you both see and hear. 34. For David did not ascend into the heavens, but he himself says,

> ' The Lord said to my Lord,
> " Sit at my right hand,
35. until I make your enemies your
>   footstool."'

36. Therefore let the entire house of Israel know with certainty that God has made him both Lord and Messiah, this Jesus whom you crucified."

But Peter's argument here seems to be incomprehensible, as the treatment by modern commentators show.[13] The general course of Peter's argument from Scripture appears to be this: (1) David said God will not allow his "Holy One" to experience corruption (2.27), and David was talking of Jesus. (2) David died and was buried, and it is emphasized that his tomb was still extant (2.29). Hence David was not the "Holy One." (3) Because David was a prophet, he knew that God would put one of his descendants on his throne (2.30). That is, David who is dead and buried and was a prophet could not have been speaking of himself at 2.27 but of one of his descendants. (4) Accordingly, Peter next changes David's second-person language at 2.27 to have him using the third person at 2.31 of the Messiah, who is Jesus, who was raised from the dead (2.32). (5) Peter then uses the same verse, Psalm 110.1, found in Luke 20.44, to prove that David was not the Messiah (2.32f.) but that Jesus is (2.36).

Thus, the evangelist Luke uses the same verse, Psalm 110.1, to prove at Luke 20.44 that the Messiah *will not* be a descendant of David and at Acts 2.34f. to prove that the Messiah *will* be a descendant of David. In Luke, the evangelist missed the point of Jesus' argument that is set out in Mark. Still, the argument from the psalm to show that Jesus was the Messiah was strong in Christian tradition. Hence Luke used it that way in Acts. Since there was strong scriptural authority that the Messiah would be a descendant of David,[14] and since that seems to have been the evangelist's position (Luke 3.23ff.), now in Acts he displays some confusion about the meaning of Jewish tradition.

For us in the present context, however, the main interest is in an episode that is partially discussed in chapter 12, the trial of Jesus before the Sanhedrin. Luke the evangelist apparently did not understand the court's procedure. According to the Mishnah Sanhedrin, the first stage of a capital trial involved a full investigation, with a decision of acquittal or of guilt.

Mishnah Sanhedrin 4.5. If they found him innocent they set him free; otherwise they leave his sentence over until the morrow. [In the meantime] they went together in pairs, they ate a little (but they used to drink no wine the whole day), and they discussed the matter all night, and early on the morrow they came to the court. He that favoured acquittal says: "I declared him innocent [yesterday] and I still declare him innocent"; and he that favoured conviction says, "I declared him guilty [yesterday] and I still declare him guilty." He that had favoured conviction may now acquit, but he that had favoured acquittal may not retract and favour conviction.

In Luke, Jesus was arrested at night (Luke 22.47ff.) and they took him illegally to the house of the high priest (Luke 22.54), not to the place of assembly.[15] At that house those who held him mocked and beat him (Luke 22.63), another breach of pretrial procedure. But there was no meeting of the Sanhedrin, no decision of guilt or acquittal, and no subsequent discussion of the issue. Instead, the assembly met in the morning (Luke 22.66ff.). To the question, "Are you, then, the Son of God?" Jesus replied, "You say that I am" (Luke 22.70).

> Luke 22.71. Then they said, "What further testimony do we need? We have heard it ourselves from his own lips."

At that stage, the assembly took Jesus before Pilate with accusations (Luke 23.1). The Lukan account of the trial is very different from that in Mark (Mark 14.53ff.), and for some scholars the differences are to be accounted for not by the use of another source but by Lukan theology.[16] Jerome Neyrey claims: "Luke's purpose [is] to describe a solemn, valid, and formal trial of Jesus by Israel."[17] If this correctly states Luke's theological intention, then Luke demonstrates his ignorance of the Sanhedrin's procedure. The trial was certainly neither formal nor valid, and in a real sense it was scarcely a trial at all. We are not told that the Sanhedrin reached a final verdict of guilty, which it should have done only after a second session. If it did, it should have carried out the execution. Instead, the members took Jesus to Pilate not as a convicted criminal but as a person accused: to be tried by the Romans.

I have discussed these matters in Luke's Gospel for any light they may shed on the use of history, or more likely of Christian tradition, by the evangelist Luke in Acts. They demonstrate that the evangelist's knowledge of Jewish ritual, custom, and practice was shaky.[18] Nonetheless, he was to some considerable extent bound by current traditions of what had happened. The main point that I want to make is that we can accept that the evangelist could make mistakes in the early chapters of Acts without drawing the conclusion that he was not relying mainly on established tradition. Thus, Luke's account of Jesus before the Sanhedrin is most implausible, but he does make the Jewish leadership responsible for Jesus' execution by the Romans. That the Jewish leadership was much involved with Jesus' execution is confirmed by Matthew and Mark. If we did not have their testimony, we might be tempted to throw out altogether Luke's view that the Jews were involved. For the early chapters of Acts we have no outside testimony: that does not mean that, because the evangelist makes some mistakes, he was wholly inventive, ignoring early Christian tradition.

Now we come specifically to the early chapters of Acts. In the first trial of Peter and John before the Sanhedrin (4.1ff.), Annas is mistakenly described as the high priest (4.6).[19] Not too much need be made of this mistake because he did hold that office from A.D. 6 to 15 and would have remained powerful, especially if as John relates (John 18.13) he was the father-in-law of Caiaphas, who then was the high priest from around 17 to 36.[20] Nor is it too significant that the arrest is said to have been made by "the priests, the captain of the Temple, and the Sadducees" (4.1). No doubt, without other members of the Sanhedrin, they had no power to arrest, but they would be regarded as the traditional enemies of the early Christians because they denied resurrection.[21] It is entirely plausible that they took the leading role in the arrests for the reason stated at verse 2, that Peter and John were teaching that in Jesus there was resurrection of the body.

At the second trial of Peter and John, Gamaliel intervenes on the side of moderation. He talks of the failed insurrections of Theudas and then, after him, of Judas in the days of the census (5.36f.). But the insurrection of Theudas was in the time of the procurator, Cuspius Fadus, around 44,[22] long after the date of this trial, so it cannot have been mentioned by Gamaliel. On the other hand, the insurrection of Judas did occur at the time of (and because of) the census of A.D. 6.[23] For our purposes the most we can deduce from this is that the evangelist's grasp of Jewish history could be as shaky as his knowledge of Jewish customs and practices. We cannot deduce that tradition did not involve an intervention of Gamaliel, far less that there was no trial of Peter and John.[24]

In the speech of Stephen there is further historical confusion. At 7.16 the bodies of the patriarchs were carried back to Shechem and laid in the tomb that Abraham had bought from the sons of Hamor in Shechem. Abraham had bought a tomb (Genesis 23), but it was Jacob who bought a tomb from the sons of Hamor in Shechem (Genesis 33.19).[25] Again, the error is no evidence against the general tradition of Stephen's speech.[26]

Paul in later Acts is depicted notoriously differently from Paul in the Epistles. Haenchen roundly declares: "Acts draws a *picture of relations between Jews and Christians which contradicts that of the Pauline epistles.*" He adds, "The representation of Paul in Acts . . . shows that here we have no collaborator of Paul telling his story, but someone of a later generation trying in his own way to give an account of things that can no longer be viewed in their true perspective."[27]

Luke, at best, was not always accurate. Still, I have been arguing, the inaccuracies do not entail a failure on Luke's part to report the living tradition of the early Christians. To the tradition I will return shortly. But I should like to raise the impossible issue of whether Stephen actually did make a speech of the kind that Luke relates. Two arguments are usually adduced against historical truth.

The first argument is that it is implausible that Stephen would be allowed to make a speech without interruption for so long when that speech was at the same time irrelevant for his defense and inflammatory. The argument has force, but it is not conclusive. To begin with, in history it is not always the plausible that occurs. Then, I have argued, the speech is by no means irrelevant, nor is it in fact long. Then we should remember the attitude ascribed to Gamaliel: some members at least of the Sanhedrin might have wanted to hear Stephen. Some might have wanted to avoid riotous behavior that could attract too much attention from the Romans. Finally, the speech did, in fact, enrage the Sanhedrin, the trial broke down in uproar, and Stephen was lynched.

The second argument against historicity is that Greek and Roman historians habitually made up speeches. This is certainly true. For Stephen's speech we should note the general difficulty that no one would have taken down full notes. At the very best, any speech would not be in the actual words of Stephen. Still, there are problems in categorically denying any historicity to Stephen's speech. There is doubt as to how far and in what sense Luke should be regarded as a standard historian. And Greek and Roman historians differed among themselves as to the approach they should take.[28] For example, the classical starting point for discussion, Thucydides *History of the Peloponnesian War* 1.22, is notoriously ambiguous or difficult to translate. In addition, the gravest doubts on the historicity of Stephen's speech often seem to spring from a misunderstanding of what the speech is about. The passage of Dibelius that I quoted at the beginning of chapter 4 is a prime example. Finally, in this context I should like to call attention to a speech of the Roman emperor Claudius that is often adduced to illustrate the freedom which ancient historians allowed themselves in reporting speeches.

The speech in question was made by Claudius in A.D. 48. It has survived in part on a bronze inscription found in Lyons[29] and is reported in Tacitus *Annales* 11.23ff. In his capacity as censor, Claudius proposed to fill Senate vacancies with prominent citizens from the Gallic provinces. Kenneth Wellesley made a detailed comparison of the two versions, excoriates Tacitus, and claims: "The brutal fact is that only with the greatest difficulty can we find any resemblance to the original." He talks of Tacitus' bungling his task as a historian. Immediately to our purpose he records: "We can find but three themes common to the original and to the copy—the theme of the acceptance of innovation (placed first by Claudius, but last by Tacitus), that of the value of foreign immigrants, and that of the shortness of the Gallic war." He talks of the weaknesses of the copy: "These are, in the main, four: first, the entire suppression of any characteristic features of Claudius's style; second, the omission of arguments that should be there; third, the addition of others which should not be there; and, fourth, an order of topics which is neither faithful to the source nor intelligible to the reader."[30]

My response for present concerns to Tacitus' recording of Claudius' speech is rather different. Tacitus does give us all the main points of the speech: the essentials are there.[31] I would not expect him to give Claudius' actual words nor to record accurately all the details of the argumentation. If we can accept—I do not say we can—that Stephen did make a defense speech before the Sanhedrin and that Luke reports it as faithfully as Tacitus does Claudius, then we would have the very substance of the speech, but we would not have Stephen's words and not always an accurate report of his arguments.

The best we can reasonably hope for is to establish that the speech was no recent invention but was firmly fixed in early Christian tradition. I have already produced in chapter 14 one argument—which I find persuasive—that Stephen's trial and speech go back to an earlier Christian tradition: one charge against him, to which he vigorously responded, was that Jesus would destroy the Temple. The accusation and defense would be pointless after A.D. 70 when the Romans, not Jesus, destroyed the Temple; hence the accusation and defense must be earlier. More than that, for Christians after 70, Stephen's belief would be wrong. It would not be a Christian invention, because it is damaging to faith. Indeed, it is a testimony to the force of the tradition that this part of Stephen's defense survived at all. It is noteworthy that only in the present context is any early Christian shown as claiming that Jesus would destroy the Temple.[32] But in the earliest days such a claim could seem plausible.

A second argument for an early tradition for the speech arises from this: the charges against Stephen are surprising. The accusation is not that Stephen was proclaiming Jesus as the Messiah, but relates to specifics. The first charge, of course, was that Stephen claimed Jesus would destroy the Temple. The other specific charge was that Stephen claimed Jesus would change the customs of Moses (6.14). I suggested in chapter 6 that at 7.37 Stephen indirectly admitted the charge and repeated the claim. I also argued in chapter 2 that the charge would seem reasonable. Yet now I would like to suggest that Jesus' changing the law was not an idea prominent in the earliest Christian thinking nor in early tradition except with regard to Stephen.[33] If my suggestion is plausible, then we have another argument to support the view that the tradition about Stephen was early.

The argument in favor of the suggestion comes from Acts 10.9ff.:

About noon the next day, as they were on their journey and approaching the city, Peter went up on the roof to pray. 10. He became hungry and wanted something to eat; and while it was being prepared, he fell into a trance. 11. He saw the heaven opened and something like a large sheet coming down, being lowered to the ground by its four corners. 12. In it were all kinds of four-footed creatures and reptiles and birds of the air. 13. Then he heard a voice saying, "Get up, Peter; kill and eat." 14. But Peter said, "By no means, Lord; for I have never eaten anything that is profane or unclean." 15. The voice said to him again, a second time, "What God has made clean, you must not call profane." 16. This happened three times, and the thing was suddenly taken up to heaven.

Peter was either unaware that Jesus had declared all food clean (Mark 7.14ff.; Matthew 15.10ff.)[34] or nonetheless so kept the Levitical rules that he was surprised when he was urged to kill and eat other things. Such surprise would be natural. After all, Jesus had not commanded the eating of food formerly prohibited, but now permitted, and in Israel of the time it would not be too easy to acquire such food: In any event the passage indicates some lack of emphasis on legal change made by Jesus.[35]

A final argument for holding that Stephen's speech goes back to an early tradition relates to curious aspects of inconsistencies in Luke-Acts. If we regard Luke-Acts as a unit with respect to Luke's beliefs, the works would reveal serious contradictions. These contradictions disappear only if we hold that different parts of Luke-Acts represent for the time involved different parts of Christian tradition (no doubt with Lukan emendations). Thus, the contents of the Gospel of Luke would derive from some strands of early Christian tradition, recorded faithfully by the evangelist Luke. Luke then used other early traditions for the first part of Acts, at least as far as the end of chapter 7. At some point in Acts—a point I leave indefinite—other strands of the traditions prevail. Beliefs held about Jesus and his message then reflect the particular tradition determined by timing and may vary from one part of Luke-Acts to another.

The clearest example of this relates to whether Jesus' message was to the Jews alone or also to the Gentiles. The decision has clear implications for Jesus' role as the Messiah. In later Acts the mission is to Gentiles as well.[36] This, indeed, is first represented as the conclusion drawn by Peter after he is told to kill and eat food he considered unclean. He was summoned to visit a centurion, Cornelius:

> Acts 10.25. On Peter's arrival Cornelius met him, and falling at his feet, worshipped him. 26. But Peter made him get up, saying, "Stand up; I am only a mortal." 27. And as he talked with him, he went in and found that many had assembled; 28. and he said to them, "You yourselves know that it is unlawful for a Jew to associate with or to visit a Gentile; but God has shown me that I should not call anyone profane or unclean. 29. So when I was sent for, I came without objection. Now may I ask why you sent for me?"

In contrast, in early Acts Jesus' message is simply assumed to be to the Jews, as it is in Luke.[37]

Similarly, the different uses made of Psalm 110.1 at Luke 21.41ff. and Acts 2.34ff. make sense on the basis that the evangelist used different strands of the traditions coming from different historical levels, though deriving ultimately from the same even earlier tradition. The version used in Luke concerned what Jesus said, that in Acts what Peter said.

On this basis, of a tradition from a particular time frame in very early Christianity, the accusations against Stephen and his defense make sense. The accusation that Jesus would destroy the Temple is incongruous for any later time. So is Stephen's emphasis on Jewishness, on exile and slavery, on disobedience to the law, and on Jews blocking the return of the Messiah.

16

✛

THE

AFTERMATH

✛ ✛ ✛

JESUS BELIEVED HE WAS THE MESSIAH, AND HE CAME TO Jerusalem expecting to be stoned to death after conviction by the Sanhedrin. He was also very much in the mold of the prophet Isaiah. But how exactly he saw himself as the Messiah is not at all clear. In no act or saying did he show himself hostile to the Roman occupation. His apocalyptic "cleansing of the Temple," carrying the traditions of Isaiah much further, was an affront to organized Judaism. But thereafter he had no strategy, and he simply waited for events to run their course.[1]

He won very few followers until just before he came to Jerusalem. With his arrest even his close disciples faded away. Still, his disciples came to believe that he rose from the dead, was the Messiah, and at that—at least for those we know about—he was the political Messiah who would return the exiles to Israel and drive out the Romans. But for this, the repentance of the Jews was necessary, and repentance meant accepting that Jesus was the Messiah. Only with that repentance would he return to earth and carry out his destiny. The first Christians were, therefore, of necessity missionaries. Peter tried persuasion. In front of the Sanhedrin Stephen was confrontational and was lynched.

Stephen's speech, whatever his intention and as it is recorded in tradition, set the scene for the future and is pivotal. Thereafter, there is no talk of Christians holding all property in common. Nor is the Second Coming of Jesus regarded as inevitably imminent. It could not be, because the Jews had rejected Jesus. But the speech is much more. The Jews had broken their covenant with God. Though they were circumcised in the flesh, they were "uncircumcised in heart and ears." There is a corollary. At that time Judaism was a religion that had great attraction for many who were not born Jews.[2] Our sources stress the presence of acolytes and God-fearers. But if circumcised Jews might be uncircumcised before God, might it be that those who were circumcised in heart and ears but uncircumcised in the flesh were truly circumcised before God? Implicitly, but nonetheless in reality, the speech of Stephen laid the foundations for the view that Gentiles did not need physical circumcision to be converted to Judaism.[3] Because of the persecution in Jerusalem that followed Stephen's death, the Christians scattered throughout Judea and Samaria (8.1) and took the message of Jesus to non-Jews and first to the Samaritans (8.4ff.).

Stephen's speech also carried the war to the Jews. For Stephen, traditional Judaism and the new Christian sect could not coexist. Traditional Judaism was the obstacle that prevented the coming of the Messiah. Unconverted Jews, thus, could not regard the Christians simply as Jews like themselves but holding some particular beliefs as did the Pharisees or Essenes. Whether or not the Jews should be regarded as the aggressors in the arrest of Stephen—and we know nothing about the previous tone of his teaching—Christianity was on the attack, at least in the person of Stephen. The battle for faith had to be won before the next battle—for freedom from the Romans—could begin.

The Romans, who are not mentioned in the early chapters of Acts, are to be regarded as always there. Though the teaching of the first Christians was directed toward the "conversion" of the Jews, it was a present danger for Jews. Conversion on a large scale would bring reprisals from the Romans. Conversion was in part—but a real part—a political statement of open enmity to Roman rule. The great majority of Jews who were not converted had little choice but to try somehow to put down the movement.

The choices for the Christians after Stephen were limited. Faced with hostility from other Jews, they could admit they were wrong or reframe their conception of the Messiah. Those we know about chose the latter. After all, so far as the surviving tradition goes, Jesus had not been anti-Roman. Indeed, Stephen's speech is the final stage, so far as our sources go, of the concept of Jesus as the political Messiah. Jesus did not claim that for himself. The apostles claimed it for him. But the idea died with the lynching of Stephen.

There is stunning irony in the trial of Stephen and its aftermath. The stress on the charges against Stephen is not that he claimed Jesus was the Messiah but that he claimed Jesus would destroy the Temple and change the law. This stress, I believe, is in the early tradition about Stephen, and it explains a great deal.

First, it explains the Romans' absence from the scene. They would be directly interested in any claim that X was the political Messiah. But Jesus, even as Messiah, was supremely apolitical with regard to the Romans. Stephen had stressed that Jesus as Messiah would destroy the Temple and alter Mosaic law. The Romans could not have cared less about such matters. The attitude of Gallio, proconsul of Achaia, with regard to Paul is instructive:

> Acts 18.12. But when Gallio was proconsul of Achaia, the Jews made a united attack on Paul and brought him before the tribunal. 13. They said, "This man is persuading people to worship God in ways that are contrary to the law." 14. Just as Paul was about to speak, Gallio said to the Jews, "If it were a matter of crime or serious villainy, I would be justified in accepting the complaint of you Jews; 15. but since it is a matter of questions about words and names and your own law, see to it yourselves; I do not wish to be a judge of these matters." 16. And he dismissed them from the tribunal.

Second, it explains the much greater anger of the Jews against Stephen than against Peter and John. To preach Jesus as Messiah as Peter and John did was wrongheaded and could cause trouble. To preach the destruction of the Temple and the alteration of the law as Stephen did was to strike at the very roots of Jewish identity and was intolerable even to splinter groups like the Essenes. For the same reasons the Sanhedrin did not involve the Romans: the matter was of no concern to the Romans but of intense importance to the Jews. The contrast with the trial of Jesus is marked. The

Sanhedrin could fear the anger of the crowd if it executed Jesus, and could fear the wrath of the Romans if Jesus were widely regarded as the Messiah and rioting followed. So the Sanhedrin involved the Romans in Jesus' death.

Third, it helps to explain the structure of Stephen's speech. He could not deny the accusations made against him, but he sought to defang them by stressing instead Jesus' role as the political Messiah. In this way the speech has misled subsequent commentators.

But why did Stephen claim that Jesus would destroy the Temple and change the law of Moses? Jews opposed the earliest Christians not only because they taught that Jesus was the Messiah but because many Jews believed Jesus had claimed that he would destroy the Temple. Stephen met this opposition head on, accepted the belief as true, and claimed the Temple was contrary to God's wishes.

The irony, of course, is that so far as our sources go, other early Christians did not emphasize that Jesus would destroy the Temple and change the law. But Stephen's outlandish preaching, as a prominent Christian, caused Jewish wrath to fall on all. No Gamaliel appeared, as at the trial of Peter and John, to plead for Stephen. And Christians or proto-Christians seem to be missing from the Sanhedrin.

The irony is greater still. Stephen was not an apostle. He has no history, unlike Peter and John. He appears from nowhere, as one of the seven Greek-speaking Jews appointed to supervise the food distribution (6.5). He did "great wonders and signs," we are told (6.8), but Luke does not seem to know what these were. Still, Stephen brought disaster upon the Christians and was at the same time perhaps the first heretic.[4]

ABBREVIATIONS

✢　✢　✢

Anchor Bible Dictionary, 1–6	*The Anchor Bible Dictionary,* 6 vols., ed. David Noel Freedman (New York, 1992).
Arichea, *Stephen Speech*	Daniel Castillo Arichea, *A Critical Analysis of the Stephen Speech in the Acts of the Apostles* (Duke University Ph.D., 1965; microfilmed by University Microfilms, Ann Arbor).
Barrett, *Acts*, 1	C. K. Barrett, *The Acts of the Apostles*, vol. 1 (Edinburgh, 1994).
Bauernfeind, *Apostelgeschichte*	Otto Bauernfeind, *Kommentar und Studien zur Apostelgeschichte* (Tübingen, 1980).
Bihler, *Stephanusgeschichte*	Johannes Bihler, *Die Stephanusgeschichte* (Munich, 1963).
Conzelmann, *Acts*	Hans Conzelmann, *Acts of the Apostles*, trans. James Limburg et al. (Philadelphia, 1987).

Daube, *New Testament*	David Daube, *The New Testament and Rabbinic Judaism* (London, 1956).
Delebecque, *Actes*	E. Delebecque, *Les Actes des Apôtres* (Paris, 1982).
Dibelius, *Studies*	Martin Dibelius, *Studies in the Acts of the Apostles*, ed. Heinrich Greeven (New York, 1956).
Haenchen, *Acts*	Ernst Haenchen, *The Acts of the Apostles, a Commentary*, trans. Bernard Noble and Gerald Shin (Oxford, 1921).
Loisy, *Actes*	Alfred Loisy, *Les Actes des Apôtres* (Paris, 1920).
Lüdemann, *Early Christianity*	Gerd Lüdemann, *Early Christianity according to the Traditions in Acts* (Minneapolis, 1989).
Munck, *Acts*	Johannes Munck, *The Acts of the Apostles*, rev. William F. Albright and C. S. Mann (Garden City, N.Y., 1967).
Neil, *Acts*	William Neil, *Acts* (Grand Rapids, 1973).
New Jerome	*The New Jerome Biblical Commentary*, ed. Raymond E. Brown et al. (Englewood Cliffs, N.J., 1990).
Roloff, *Apostelgeschichte*	Jürgen Roloff, *Die Apostelgeschichte*, 17th ed. (Göttingen, 1981).
Sanders, *Judaism*	E. P. Sanders, *Judaism: Practice and Belief, 63 B.C.E.–66 C.E.* (Philadelphia, 1992).

Scharlemann, *Stephen*	Martin H. Scharlemann, *Stephen: A Singular Saint*, (Rome, 1968).
Schiffmann, *Reclaiming*	Lawrence H. Schiffmann, *Reclaiming the Dead Sea Scrolls* (Philadelphia, 1994).
Schmithals, *Apostelgeschichte*	Walter Schmithals, *Die Apostelgeschichte des Lukas* (Zurich, 1982).
Schneider, *Apostelgeschichte*	Gerhard Schneider, *Die Apostelgeschichte*, vol. 1 (Freiburg, 1980).
Shanks, *Christianity*	*Christianity and Rabbinic Judaism*, ed. Hershel Shanks (Washington, D.C., 1992).
Simon, *St. Stephen*	Marcel Simon, *St. Stephen and the Hellenists in the Early Church* (London, 1958).
Strack-Billerbeck, *Kommentar* 1, 2	Hermann L. Strack and Paul Billerbeck, *Kommentar zum Neuen Testament aus Talmud und Midrasch*, vol. 1, 5th ed. (Munich, 1969); vol. 2, 4th ed. (Munich, 1965).
Trocmé, *Actes*	Etienne Trocmé, *Le "Livre des Actes" et l'histoire* (Paris, 1957).
Watson, *Jesus and the Jews*	Alan Watson, *Jesus and the Jews: The Pharisaic Tradition in John* (Athens, Ga., 1995).
Watson, *Law*	Alan Watson, *Jesus and the Law* (Athens, Ga., 1996).
Watson, *Trial*	Alan Watson, *The Trial of Jesus* (Athens, Ga., 1995).
Wikenhauser, *Apostelgeschichte*	Alfred Wikenhauser, *Die Apostelgeschichte*, 3d ed. (Regensburg, 1956).

Williams, *Acts*

David J. Williams, *Acts: New International Biblical Commentary* (1990, Peabody).

Williams, *Commentary*

C. S. C. Williams, *A Commentary on the Acts of the Apostles* (New York, 1957).

NOTES

PREFACE

1. But the word μάρτυς is not used of Stephen with the sense of martyr. When it occurs in Acts 22.20 it has its usual New Testament meaning of witness: cf. G. W. Bowersock, *Martyrdom and Rome* (Cambridge, 1995), 75.

2. I admit also to some disquiet. A major preoccupation of Roman law scholars and of writers on Acts is the uncovering of the levels of sources in our existing texts. But for the opening chapters of Acts—with which we are concerned—there is no outside control. If scholars reject the relevancy of Stephen's speech as they do, then it seems to me quite pointless, because impossible, to attempt to determine the extent to which the speech is a Lukan invention or is based on early traditions. The consequent diversity of opinions with no convincing conclusion is brought out in the quotation from Haenchen given in chapter 14.

3. An outstanding full modern commentary is Barrett, *Acts*, 1.

1 BACKGROUND TO THE STEPHEN AFFAIR IN ACTS

1. See, e.g., Emil Schürer, *The History of the Jewish People in the Age of Jesus Christ*, 2d ed., eds. Geza Vermes and Fergus Millar (Edinburgh,

1973), 1:243ff.; Louis H. Feldman in Shanks, *Christianity*, 2ff.; Fergus Millar, *The Roman Near East, 31 B.C.-A.D. 337* (Cambridge, 1993), 42ff.

2. This is argued from the fact that until A.D. 36 the garments of the high priest that had to be worn on such and other occasions were kept in the Roman fortress, the Antonia, under a triple seal, one of which was that of the commander of the Roman garrison: Josephus *Antiquities* 15.403ff., 18.90ff., 20.6f. For issues of the composition of the Sanhedrin see Feldman in Shanks, *Christianity*, 7ff.

3. Josephus *Antiquities* 17.355, 18.2ff., 18.9ff.; *War* 2.118, 2.433; Philo *Embassy to Gaius*. For the Zealots see, e.g., Martin Hengel, *The Zealots*, trans. David Smith (Edinburgh, 1989).

4. See, e.g., Schmithals, *Apostelgeschichte*, 61; Feldman in Shanks, *Christianity*, 13.

5. See Sanders, *Judaism*, 318ff., 323ff., 332ff. See, Josephus *Antiquities* 14.175 for the conduct of Herod killing all the members of the Sanhedrin.

6. For Jewish groups see Josephus *War* 2.119ff.; *Antiquities* 18.9ff.; infra, chapter 3.

7. For the views of the majority see, e.g., Sanders, *Judaism*, 119ff.

8. See, e.g., Feldman in Shanks, *Christianity*, 6ff.; and the essays in *The Messiah: Developments in Earliest Judaism and Christianity*, ed. James H. Charlesworth (Minneapolis, 1987).

9. For my argument see Watson, *Law*, 111ff.

10. For my own views, see Watson, *Trial*, 150ff. The sources are unanimous and are not solely Christian: Matthew 27.24ff.; Mark 15.12ff.; Luke 23.13ff.; John 19.1ff.; Josephus *Antiquities* 18.63f.; Tacitus *Annales* 15.44. We need not spend space on those modern commentators who, despite the evidence of the sources, know "what must have been." Some modern examples are Simon Légasse, *Le procès de Jésus 1. L'histoire* (Paris, 1994); Enoch Powell, *The Evolution of the Gospel: A New Translation of the First Gospel* (New Haven, 1994); John D. Crossan, *Who Killed Jesus?* (San Francisco, 1995).

11. Matthew 28; Mark 16; Luke 24; John 20, 21; Acts 1.1–11.

12. Cf., e.g., Trocmé, *Actes*, 189; Simon, *St. Stephen*, 9ff.

13. See, e.g., Robert Grant, *A Historical Introduction to the New Testament* (London, 1963), 133ff.; Munck, *Acts*, xvff.; Williams, *Acts*, 2ff.; Conzelmann, *Acts*, xxviiff.; Bauernfeind, *Apostelgeschichte*, 11f.

14. For the significance and argument see Watson, *Trial*, 143ff.

15. Watson, *Trial*, 20ff., 53ff., 66ff.

16. For the nature of the Messiah see, e.g., Sanders, *Judaism*, 289ff.; Schiffman, *Reclaiming*, 317ff.

17. Munck, *Acts*, 7. Bauernfeind thinks the kingdom is "the Israel of God" rather than the earthly kingdom: *Apostelgeschichte*, 21ff.; cf. Schmithals, *Apostelgeschichte*, 21f.; Schneider, *Apostelgeschichte*, 1:201. Barrett says: "Luke uses the question to underline the nonnationalist character of the Christian movement; the disciples asked it (thus by failure to perceive the truth eliciting the positive statement of v. 8)": *Acts*, 1:76.

18. Wikenhauser, *Apostelgeschichte*, 27. For Roloff, Luke knew that in the earliest days of the Christian community Jesus' resurrection was understood to be the direct beginning of the "end-events": *Apostelgeschichte*, 23. A different explanation is given by Haenchen, *Acts*, 143. For him the question is not about the disciples' ignorance. Rather, it highlights the problem of the expected end of the world, linked with the question of whether the kingdom was restricted to Israel. This seems far removed from the wording of the question, which is about the "restoration of the kingdom," not about the end of the world, and "to Israel."

19. For Pentecost see, e.g., Barrett, *Acts*, 1:110ff.

20. For the list of nations, see Conzelmann, *Acts*, 14.

21. For a discussion of the problems and views that have been held see Haenchen, *Acts*, 167ff.

22. On the use of Joel see Barrett, *Acts*, 1:135ff.

23. It should be stressed that there is no evidence that the very earliest Christians—the apostles—expected the end of the world to be imminent. Paul is a different story: 1 Corinthians 5.29f., 15.51f.; 1 Thessalonians 4.16f. For eschatology and Jesus see Amos N. Wilder, *Eschatology and Ethics in the Teaching of Jesus*, 2d ed. (New York, 1950), especially at 37ff. Jesus himself, it should be emphasized, is not represented in the Gospels as being interested in secular politics: cf. Watson, *Trial*, 30f., 34ff., 48f., 151.

24. See Conzelmann, who does not believe the account is historical: *Acts*, 24. Haenchen argues, perhaps plausibly, that the property was shared, not disposed of, and whenever there was need of money for the poor of the congregation one of the property owners sold his piece of land or valuables: *Acts*, 192. But that is clearly contrary to Acts 4.32, 4.34. The texts are not unanimous: cf., e.g., Jacques Dupont, *Nouvelles Etudes sur les Actes des Apôtres* (Paris, 1984), 299ff. See also Barrett, *Acts*, 1:162ff.

25. See Wikenhauser, *Apostelgeschichte*, 61.

26. Again for Haenchen the speech is about the second advent: *Acts*, 210. But he does find singular "the idea of the hastening of the second advent through the conversion of the Jews."

27. Cf. Sirach 36.13; Baruch 4.36f., 5.5; 2 Maccabees 1.27f., 2.18; Book of Jubilees 1.15; Psalms of Solomon 8.34, 11.2f., 17.28ff., 17.50; Temple Scroll of Qumran 8.14ff., 57.5f.

28. See A. A. di Lella, s.v. "Wisdom of Ben Sirah" in *Anchor Bible Dictionary*, 6:934.

29. See Joseph L. Trafton, s.v. "Solomon, Psalms of" in *Anchor Bible Dictionary*, 6:115.

30. Cf. Sirach 36.1ff.; Book of Jubilees 24.29f.; Third Sibylline Oracle 3.670ff., 3.709. For a modern theological interpretation see Barrett, *Acts*, 1:202ff.

31. For what is looked to as not the end of the universe but a new order see E. P. Sanders in Shanks, *Christianity*, 57f. The Qumran community's longing for the "End of Days" was for their victory over all others, not for the end of the world. They expected two Messiahs, one with priestly, the other with temporal, rule: see Schiffman, *Reclaiming*, 321ff., 329ff., 391ff.; Sanders, *Judaism*, 295ff.

32. For Bauernfeind, the prophet of verses 22f. is Jesus in his lifetime: *Apostelgeschichte*, 69.

33. Josephus *Antiquities* 18.16f.; Matthew 22.23.

34. Cf. Sanders, *Judaism*, 317ff.; Schiffman, *Reclaiming*, 73ff.

35. See Munck, *Acts*, 31f.; Williams, *Acts*, 77f.; Conzelmann, *Acts*, 31ff.; Haenchen, *Acts*, 215; Bauernfeind, *Apostelgeschichte*, 72ff.; Roloff, *Apostelgeschichte*, 81f.

36. See Sanders, *Judaism*, 458ff.

37. Josephus *War* 2.163; *Antiquities* 18.14. For the Pharisees see Sanders, *Judaism*, 380ff.; Schiffman, *Reclaiming*, 76ff.

38. But the crime with which they were charged is not at all clear: see the discussion in Haenchen, *Acts*, 221ff. Haenchen acutely observes that the apostles were arrested only after Peter's sermon, not immediately after the miracle. My own suggestion, though I will not insist upon it, is that Peter's claim that salvation comes only from Jesus was the crime of leading a town astray. The penalty for this was death by stoning: Mishnah Sanhedrin 7.4.

39. See, e.g., Bauernfeind, *Apostelgeschichte*, 91ff.

40. For Gamaliel see Bruce Chilton and the bibliography that he gives, s.v. "Gamaliel" in *Anchor Bible Dictionary*, 2:904ff.; cf. Bauernfeind, *Apostelgeschichte*, 94ff.; Barrett, *Acts*, 1:292f. The historical errors in his speech are discussed infra, chapter 15.

41. For discussion see Haenchen, *Acts*, 239ff.

42. Lüdemann, *Early Christianity*, 74f.

43. See Strack-Billerbeck, *Kommentar*, 2:643ff.; Joachim Jeremias, *Jerusalem in the Time of Jesus* (Philadelphia, 1969), 131.

44. Acts 2.42, 2.46.

45. See Jeremias, *Jerusalem*, 131.

46. We need not decide whether the Jewish Christians at this time still received the standard Jewish dole, but see, e.g., Lüdemann, *Early Christianity*, 75f.

47. See Munck, *Acts*, 56f.; Conzelmann, *Acts*, 45; Neil, *Acts*, 102; Haenchen, *Acts*, 260ff.; Schmithals, *Apostelgeschichte*, 64f.; Schneider, *Apostelgeschichte*, 420ff. A full discussion of theories is in Arichea, *Stephen Speech*, 112ff. See also C. S. Mann in Munck, *Acts*, 301ff.; Lüdemann, *Early Christianity*, 78f.

48. For Bauernfeind, the complaint was justified, though Luke avoids blaming the apostles: *Apostelgeschichte*, 100.

49. See J. W. Packer, *Acts of the Apostles* (Cambridge, 1966), 50; Lüdemann, *Early Christianity*, 77; Haenchen, *Acts*, 264ff. A puzzle, which is not of direct relevance in this book, is that one of them, Nicolaus, was not a Jew but a proselyte: cf. Trocmé, *Actes*, 189. For the names see Barrett, *Acts*, 1:314f. For proselytes see Feldman in Shanks, *Christianity*, 28ff.

50. But his prominent position on the list may be because of his notorious subsequent trial. For Roloff, that Stephen is named first shows his leading position among the Hellenists: *Apostelgeschichte*, 110.

51. Conzelmann, *Acts*, 44. See also Loisy, *Actes*, 305.

52. Delebecque does, however, seem to take it literally in some sense: *Actes*, 28. He assumes that up to this time women—not the apostles—had been the servers, but the growing number of recipients had made the task too heavy. But the opposition in his "women—Stephen and the other six," rather than "the apostles—Stephen and the other six" is arbitrary and not supported by the text. Wikenhauser also thinks the seven were appointed to table service and that that task was not previously performed by the apostles: *Apostelgeschichte*, 78f., 196ff.

2 STEPHEN ACCUSED

1. For a discussion of one or more synagogues see, e.g., Williams, *Commentary*, 99; Neil, *Acts*, 105; Loisy, *Actes*, 307f.; Lüdemann, *Early Christianity*, 82ff. For the use of Greek in Palestine see Louis H. Feldman in Shanks, *Christianity*, 19ff.

2. Philo *Embassy to Gaius* 155. Cf. Wikenhauser, *Apostelgeschichte*, 82.

3. This anger would be felt even though Stephen himself would seem from his name to be Greek. I do not see an abrupt and disjointed transition between verses 10 and 11 as Arichea does: *Stephen Speech*, 161. For the idea of conflict between converted and unconverted Greek-speaking Jews see, e.g., Trocmé, *Actes*, 187.

4. Loisy, *Actes*, 305–6.

5. Haenchen, *Acts*, 267–68. See also Simon, *St. Stephen*, 4ff.

6. Bihler, *Stephanusgeschichte*, 10.

7. Cf. Bauernfeind, *Apostelgeschichte*, 109.

8. Cf. Lüdemann, *Early Christianity*, 85. Scharlemann suggests that the witnesses are called "false" because they brought their accusations with malice aforethought, not because they invented the substance of their changes: *Stephen*, 13. This seems unnecessary. Scharlemann also believes the false witnesses were right in accusing Stephen of saying that Jesus would destroy the Temple: *Stephen*, 51, 105ff. But for John B. Polhill, Stephen was "framed": *Acts* (Nashville, 1992), 185. Barrett talks of a "rigged" trial: *Acts*, 1:327.

9. For example, E. P. Sanders, *Jewish Law from Jesus to the Mishnah* (Philadelphia, 1990), 5.

10. Mishnah Shabbath 7.2.

11. For the distinction see, e.g., Daube, *New Testament*, 67.

12. Mishnah Yoma 8.6: "Moreover R. Mattithiah b. Heresh said: if a man has a pain in his throat they may drop medicine into his mouth on the Sabbath, since there is doubt whether life is in danger, and whenever there is doubt whether life is in danger, this overrides the Sabbath." Cf. Mishnah Shabbath 18.3.

13. For the Pharisees they would be one and the same thing. For Pharisaic observance of the law see Josephus *War* 1.110; *Antiquities* 18.12ff.; for a modern discussion see Sanders, *Judaism*, 413ff. Believing Jews, even today, have an image of a "dual Torah," written law and oral law. Written law has no primacy, but God's revelation was of both at the same time: see Babylonian Talmud B'rakot 4.b; for a modern account see Perry Dane, "The Oral Law and the Jurisprudence of a Textless Text," *S'vara* 2 (1991): 11ff.

14. For some agreement on what follows and a different perspective see E. P. Sanders in Shanks, *Christianity*, 55ff.

15. Mishnah Shekalim 6.5.

16. For the Temple tax see Mishnah Shekalim.

17. See Watson, *Jesus and the Jews*, 66ff.

18. See Matthew 24.1ff.; Luke 21.5ff. For a discussion see, e.g., Bihler, *Stephanusgeschichte*, 12ff.; cf. Roloff, *Apostelgeschichte*, 112f.; E. P. Sanders in Shanks, *Christianity*, 53f.; Schneider, *Apostelgeschichte*, 438ff.

19. The translation is from J. K. Elliott, *The Apocryphal New Testament* (Oxford, 1993), 144.

20. See, e.g., Watson, *Law*, 26ff., 32ff., 52ff., 63ff., 74ff.

21. For views on attitudes to the law at the time see Sanders, *Judaism*, 190ff., 213ff. On rabbinic sources see Feldman in Shanks, *Christianity*, 14f.

22. See Robert T. Anderson, s.v. "Samaritans" in *Anchor Bible Dictionary*, 5:940ff.

23. See also Josephus *War* 5.193ff., 2.27ff.; *Antiquities* 12.145.

24. See also Philo *Embassy to Gaius* 212.

25. *War* 6.124. For the importance of the Temple to Jews in general see Bihler, *Stephanusgeschichte*, 136ff.; Sanders, *Judaism*, 47ff.

26. Josephus *Antiquities* 18.305ff. On the whole episode see also Philo *Embassy to Gaius*. Cf. David Daube, *Civil Disobedience in Antiquity* (Edinburgh, 1972), 92ff.

27. *Antiquities* 12.43, 12.157; Sirach 50.1ff.

28. For hostility to the Temple see, e.g., Oscar Callmann, "L'Opposition contre le Temple de Jérusalem: Motif commun de la Théologie Johannique et du Monde ambiant," *New Testament Studies* 5 (1958–59): 157ff.

29. See above all John Sawyer, *The Fifth Gospel: Isaiah in the History of Christianity* (Cambridge, 1995), 1ff.; followed by Watson, *Law*, 112ff.

30. Isaiah 66.1ff.

31. Marcel Simon holds that Philo does not condemn the Temple but just does not give it the greatest importance: "Saint Stephen and the Jerusalem Temple," *Journal of Ecclesiastical History* 1 (1950): 127ff. at 134f.

32. Josephus *Antiquities* 18.18.

33. See J. J. Collins in *The Old Testament Pseudepigrapha*, ed. James H. Charlesworth (Garden City, N.Y., 1983), 1:355. Schürer suggests a date around 140 B.C.: Emil Schürer, *The History of the Jewish People in the Age of Jesus Christ (175 B.C.–A.D. 135)*, ed. Geza Vermes, Fergus Millar, Matthew Black, Martin Goodmar, and Pamela Vermes (Edinburgh, 1979), 2:501. The translation that I print is that of Collins.

34. See Collins in *Pseudepigrapha*, 357.

35. It was formulated near the end of the second century A.D. and set forth by Judah the Patriarch: see, e.g., Jacob Neusner, *The Mishnah* (New Haven, 1988), xv.

36. See Elias Bickerman, *"Imago crucis,"* in *Studies in Jewish and Christian History* (Leiden, 1986), 3:87.

37. See Raymond E. Brown, *The Death of the Messiah* (New York, 1994), 1:520ff., 532ff.

38. See, e.g., A. J. Saldanini, s.v. "Sanhedrin," in *The Anchor Bible Dictionary*, 5:978; Brown, *Death*, 1:343ff.

39. See Schürer, *History* 2:210.

40. See, e.g., Daube, *New Testament*, 303ff.

41. Cf. *The New Oxford Annotated Bible* (Oxford, 1991), 186AP.

42. See also 2 Maccabees 8.4.

43. For our purposes we need not deal with the question that has troubled many commentators of whether the Sanhedrin operated in accordance with the law as interpreted by the Pharisees: cf., e.g., Brown, *Death* 1:353ff. For us, it is enough that Jesus had also thoroughly incensed the Sadducees by his cleansing of the Temple: cf. Brown, *Death*, 1:361ff. For the charge see also J. C. O'Neill, "The Charge of Blasphemy at Jesus' Trial before the Sanhedrin," in *The Trial of Jesus*, ed. Ernst Bammel (Naperville, Ill., 1970), 72ff. For allegations of blasphemy at the trial see also Brown, *Death*, 1:534ff.

44. For the trial of Jesus I have relied on the version in Mark, partly because I believe it closest to early Jewish tradition, partly because in Luke there was really no full trial with two stages before the Sanhedrin. For my arguments see Watson, *Trial*.

3 THE ESSENES, QUMRAN, AND THE CHARGES
AGAINST STEPHEN

1. Jerusalem Talmud Sanhedrin 10.6.29c.

2. *Hypothetica* 11.1ff.; *Every Good Man Is Free* 75ff. Philo observes at § 75 that the Essenes abstained from animal sacrifice.

3. See The Community Rule (1QS) 8.9; cf. Schiffman, *Reclaiming*, 108ff. The earlier Damascus Covenant (CD) indicates that individuals owned private property; see Schiffman, *Reclaiming*, 106f.

4. The Community Rule (1QS) 6.25. The translation is that of Geza Vermes, *The Dead Sea Scrolls in English*, 4th ed. (Harmondsworth, 1995), 78; cf. Schiffman, *Reclaiming*, 108.

5. See, e.g., Trocmé, *Actes*, 197ff.

6. The Community Rule (1QS) 6.2f.; cf. Schiffman, *Reclaiming*, 334f.

7. See The Messianic Rule (1QSa) 1.22ff. (Vermes, *Scrolls*, 120f.); cf. Schiffman, *Reclaiming*, 321ff.

8. On Sabbath observance see Schiffman, *Reclaiming*, 275ff.

9. The translation is that of Vermes, *Scrolls*, 110f. It may be noted that Jesus accepted that Pharisees might rescue a sheep from a pit on the Sabbath: Matthew 12.11.

10. Vermes's translation, *Scrolls*, 117; cf. Schiffman, *Reclaiming*, 100ff.

11. *Miqṣat Ma'ase ha-Torah*, B1ff.; See, e.g., Schiffman, *Reclaiming*, 86f.

12. See, e.g., Schiffman, *Reclaiming*, 257ff. For an account of the beliefs of the community see Vermes's *Scrolls*, 41ff.

13. Apart, that is, from the Gospel of Thomas 71.

14. I have not discussed the views of the Samaritans in this chapter because, although they regarded themselves as Israelites, the Jews did not: see R. T. Anderson, s.v. "Samaritans" in *International Standard Bible Encyclopedia* (Grand Rapids, 1988), 4:303ff.

4 THE MEANING OF STEPHEN'S DEFENSE

1. Dibelius, *Studies*, 167ff. A standard view of the irrelevance of the speech will be found, for example, in F. F. Bruce, *The Book of Acts* (Grand Rapids, 1981), 141.

2. Haenchen, *Acts*, 286.

3. Wikenhauser, *Apostelgeschichte*, 86; for other views see, e.g., Scharlemann, *Stephen*, 4, and the works he cites; Roloff, *Apostelgeschichte*, 117; Marion L. Soards, *The Speeches in Acts: Their Content, Context, and Concerns* (Louisville, Ky., 1994), 57ff.

4. Also, it should not be forgotten that the Hellenistic world had a wider sense than we do of what was relevant in a speech for the defense or prosecution. In the absence of direct evidence in Israel of the time I will not go into the matter, but see in general John A. Crook, *Legal Advocacy in the Roman World* (Ithaca, N.Y., 1995), and the works he cites.

5. *The New Oxford Annotated Bible* (New York, 1977), 171NT.

6. Cf. Conzelmann, *Acts*, 51; Loisy, *Actes*, 319. For Bihler the speech is nothing but a look at the history of Israel: *Stephanusgeschichte*, 33.

7. True, this is not quite exile because Abraham had not set foot in the land, but he was promised it. The thrust, I maintain, is present.

8. Philo *Embassy to Gaius* 212; Josephus *War* 6.124.

5 STEPHEN'S SPEECH I: ABRAHAM AND JOSEPH

1. The same mode of address is found in a speech of Paul: Acts 22.1.

2. We are not concerned with the modern argument that circumcision is later as a rite with theological significance: so Gerhard von Rad, *Genesis: A Commentary*, trans. John H. Marks (Philadelphia, 1961), 335. What matters is the belief of Luke, Stephen, and his hearers.

3. Nils Alstrup Dahl, *Jesus in the Memory of the Early Church* (Minneapolis, 1976), 77.

4. Ibid., 71.

5. The same is the case with the quotation in 7.7, which derives from Septuagint Genesis 15.13f.; cf. Dahl, *Jesus*, 71; Haenchen, *Acts*, 279.

6. Conzelmann, *Acts*, 52.

7. Cf. Williams, *Acts*, 131f.

8. Singular is in the Greek. If we suspect a coded reference to conditions of Stephen's own day, then the nation is the Romans.

9. Williams says of 7.9–14, "It would appear that much of the detail of these verses is here simply for its own sake": *Acts*, 133. But he does observe that the reiteration of the word *Egypt* stresses that God is everywhere.

10. See George E. Mendenhall and Gary A. Herion, s.v. "Covenant" in *Anchor Bible Dictionary*, 1:1179ff., and the bibliography they give, 1201f.

11. See Loisy, *Actes*, 323ff.

12. Richard J. Dillon in *New Jerome*, 741.

13. Conzelmann, *Acts*, 53.

14. Roloff, *Apostelgeschichte*, 121.

15. See above all Scharlemann, *Stephen*, 68f.; cf. B. W. Butler, "Stephen's Speech: Its Argument and Doctrinal Relationship," in *Biblical and Semitic Studies* (New York, 1901), 248f.; Scobie, "Source Material," 414.

16. See, e.g., Conzelmann, *Acts*, 52; Williams, *Acts*, 134f.; Haenchen, *Acts*, 280; Lawrence E. Toombs, s.v. "Shechem (Place)" in *Anchor Bible Dictionary* 5:1183.

17. Josephus *Antiquities* 2.198ff.

6 STEPHEN'S SPEECH II: MOSES

1. Exodus 1.16 specified that only male infants were to be slaughtered. Acts 7.19 is less specific.

2. See also Josephus *Antiquities* 2.232; Philo *Life of Moses* 1.19.

3. See Strack-Billerbeck, *Kommentar*, 2:678f.; Philo *Life of Moses* 1.20ff.; and Josephus *Antiquities* 2.238.

4. See David Daube, "Neglected Nuances of Exposition in Luke-Acts," in *Aufstieg und Niedergang der römischen Welt*, ed. Hildegard Temporini and Wolfgang Haase (Berlin, 1985), 2329ff. at 2346ff. For Jesus as the new Moses in Matthew see Dale C. Allison, *The New Moses: A Matthean Typology* (Minneapolis, 1993). For Luke's high regard for Moses see Barrett, *Acts*, 1:353ff.

5. Cf. Delebecque, *Actes*, 33.

6. The bush in Greek is specifically a bramble bush in Stephen's speech, in Septuagint Exodus 3.2f., in Philo *Life of Moses* 1.67, and in the Hebrew equivalent at Exodus 3.2f. For rabbinic explanations of the choice of this bush see, e.g., Strack-Billerbeck, *Kommentar*, 2:680.

7. See, e.g., Munck, *Acts*, 63f.; Conzelmann, *Acts*, 54; Williams, *Acts*, 137f.

8. Munck, *Acts*, 63. Wikenhauser notes that the history of Moses is treated exhaustively: *Apostelgeschichte*, 89.

9. Williams, *Acts*, 138.

10. Matthew 3.13ff.; Mark 1.9ff.; Luke 3.21f. John 1.29ff. is the equivalent passage, but John does not expressly say that the Baptist baptized Jesus.

11. Cf. John 1.33f.

12. Philo *Life of Moses* 1.67.

13. Cf. Lars Hartman, s.v. "Baptism" in *Anchor Bible Dictionary*, 1:583ff.

14. Cf. Matthew 22.1ff.; Luke 20.27ff.

15. Cf. Matthew 22.31f.; Luke 20.37f.

16. See, e.g., David Daube, *Appeasement or Resistance* (Berkeley, 1987), 4ff.

17. Cf. David Daube, "Zukunftsmusik: Some Desirable Lines of Exploration in the New Testament Field," *Bulletin of the John Rylands University Library of Manchester* 68 (1985): 53ff. at 65.

18. In Matthew 3.11 John declares he is unworthy to *carry* Jesus' sandals. For a discussion see Daube, *New Testament*, 266f.

19. It should be noted, though, that at least for later rabbis a disciple should do for his teacher all that a slave should do for his owner except take off his sandals: Babylonian Talmud Ketuboth 96a:

R. Joshua b. Levi rules: All manner of service that a slave must render to his master a student must render to his teacher, except that of taking off his shoe. Rabba explained: This ruling applied only to a place where he is not known, but where he is known there can be no objection. R. Ashi said: Even where he is not known the ruling applies only where he does not put on *tefillin*, but where he puts on *tefillin* he may well perform such a service.

The translation is taken from *The Babylonian Talmud Seder Nashim*, trans. Isidore Epstein (London, 1936), 2:610. See further Daube, *New Testament*, 266f. and especially 268ff. The qualifications of Rabba and R. Ashi were to avoid the shame of a disciple being wrongly mistaken for a Gentile. If the disciple were known or wore *tefillin*, he would not be thought to be a non-Jewish slave of a Jew.

20. Cf. Williams, *Acts*, 138. Oddly, Williams sees here a subordinate theme, the parallel between Moses and Jesus, which is making its appearance for the first time. For me the theme is not subordinate and has been present from the beginning.

21. There was a tradition, which is indicated here, that an angel was involved in the transmission of the law to Moses: Septuagint Deuteronomy 33.2; Book of Jubilees 1.27ff. Cf. Williams, *Commentary*, 108; Neil, *Acts*, 115; Arichea, *Stephen Speech*, 194n. 2.

22. Williams, *Commentary*, 109. For "Babylon" as signifying Rome see E. P. Sanders in Shanks, *Christianity*, 54.

7 STEPHEN'S SPEECH III: THE JEWS' DISOBEDIENCE TO GOD

1. Exodus 25.40.

2. Cf. Williams, *Commentary*, 110; Scobie, "Source Material," 408. According to Delebecque, Stephen is prudent in expressing the idea that God does not reside in the Temple, an idea that would have been judged rash: *Actes*, 36.

3. A. F. J. Klijn, who does not believe that the speech is an attack on the Temple, gives a bibliography of those who do: "Stephen's Speech—Acts VII.2–53," *New Testament Studies* 4 (1957–58): 25ff. at 25n. 2. His own conclusion is that Stephen was executed because of the way he summarized the history of the Jews: 26f. On the Temple see also Bihler, *Stephanusgeschichte*, 71ff. For Scharlemann: "Within the Christian community Stephen took the position that any approach to the Samaritans should begin with an open rejection of the temple and its cult": *Stephen*, 187.

4. Though not necessarily germane, it may be noticed that David was perhaps not suitable because he was a man of blood, and Jerusalem as a place then of military occupation was perhaps not suitable as a place of rest for God.

5. For Simon, 2 Samuel 7 was in its original form directed against the Temple: *St. Stephen*, 53ff.

6. For a discussion see, e.g., Loisy, *Actes*, 341ff.

7. Still, it may be noted that Solomon was regarded as being not so true to God, at least in his old age, as David was: 1 Kings 11.3.

8. An alternative explanation is that Stephen or the source for this part of the speech was Samaritan, and thus the holy place was on Mount Gerizim, not the Temple in Jerusalem: for discussion and literature see Scobie, "Source Material," 399ff. But that would simply not account for the claim that *Jesus* would destroy the Temple, a belief that is met with elsewhere than in the speech of Stephen. Scobie exaggerates the role of Shechem in Acts 7. Thus, it is not mentioned at verse 45 exactly where one would expect it on a thesis of Samaritan influence. Scobie's chopping of verses into Samaritan/non-Samaritan (409ff.) seems arbitrary. For a Samaritan connection see also Schneider, *Apostelgeschichte*, 449f.; Barrett, *Acts*, 1:335, 342f., 361.

9. Cf. Delebecque, *Actes*, 37.

10. For the circumcision of hearts see also Deuteronomy 33.2; Jeremiah 4.4.

11. See Arichea, *Stephen Speech*, 203n. 4, and the works he cites; Bihler, *Stephanusgeschichte*, 77ff.

12. Cf. Delebecque, *Actes*, 37.

13. See, e.g., Acts 3.37ff.

8 STEPHEN'S DEATH

1. See, e.g., Neil, *Acts*, 116.

2. Bihler observes that scholars have often wondered whether there was a regular court procedure or riotous behavior: *Stephanusgeschichte*, 11.

3. For the argument see Watson, *Trial*, 100ff.

4. Mishnah Sanhedrin 5.5.

5. See, e.g., Exodus 17.4; Numbers 14.10; 1 Kings 12.18; 2 Chronicles 10.18; Ezekiel 16.40; John 8.59, 10.31f, 11.8; Acts 14.19.

6. Leviticus 24.14; cf. Neil, *Acts*, 118.

7. Cf. Acts 22.20.

8. Cf. Schneider, *Apostelgeschichte*, 477.

9. See, e.g., Daube, *New Testament*, 304f.

10. Cf. Daube, *New Testament*, 308ff.; Watson, *Jesus and the Jews*, 88ff.

11. Deuteronomy 17.7.

9 JESUS AND THE TEMPLE

1. See especially David Daube, *Civil Disobedience in Antiquity* (Edinburgh, 1972) 101ff.; Watson, *Jesus and the Jews*, 66ff.

2. The arguments in these next paragraphs derive for the greatest part from private letters from John Sawyer. His own powerful version appears in his book *The Fifth Gospel: Isaiah in the History of Christianity* (Cambridge, 1995).

3. See, e.g., Isaiah 1.4, 3.8, 9.13, 16ff., 29.13f., 30.12ff.

4. Isaiah 1.11. One might also postulate some hostility toward animal sacrifices in the Psalms: 40.6, 50.8f., 50.13, 51.16. Still, especially in light of Psalm 51.19, I believe a better interpretation is that sacrifices are acceptable only when offered in the proper spirit.

5. It is surprising that Jesus does not quote Isaiah.

6. Cf. Matthew 24.1ff.; Luke 21.5ff.

7. Isaiah 29.13, 1.14.

8. See also Isaiah 6.10.

9. But then there is a conflict with Matthew 17.24ff.; cf. David Daube, *Appeasement and Civil Disobedience* (Berkeley, 1987), 39ff.; Watson, *Law*, 107f.

10. See also Matthew 21.12. Luke 19.46 does not mention the buyers.

11. For Jesus and the Temple see also Bihler, *Stephanusgeschichte*, 161ff.

10 ENCODEMENT

1. Boccaccio *Terza Giornata* 3.

2. Olivia Robinson observes in writing to me that she regards this as the prime home of coded messages rather than in declarations of romantic passion and in illicit assignations. But she admits she does not have my experience.

3. Numerous examples are discussed in the Philadelphia Museum of Art exhibition catalog, *Masters of Seventeenth-Century Dutch Genre Painting* (Philadelphia, 1984).

4. John Hale, *The Civilization of the Renaissance in Europe* (New York, 1993), 83.

5. Alison Lurie, *Don't Tell the Grown-ups: Subversive Children's Literature* (Boston, 1990), passim.

6. For example, "You shall not plow with an ox and an ass yoked together": Deuteronomy 22.10. The law is convincingly explained by Calum Carmichael, *Women, Law, and the Genesis Traditions* (Edinburgh, 1979), 33. The law relates to responses to Shechem's seduction of Jacob's daughter Dinah: Genesis 34. Shechem, whose name means "ass," is slaughtered by Jacob's sons. Jacob says of these sons, "In their anger they killed men and at their whim they hamstrung oxen": Genesis 49.6. "Oxen" refers to Jacob's family, and the term is used elsewhere of the Israelites. "To plow" often has a sexual significance. Thus, the law prohibits a sexual liaison between an Israelite and a Hivite (as Shechem was). Joseph Blenkinsopp's suggestion in *New Jerome*, 1–4, that the law was perhaps to spare the weaker animal is unconvincing: the suggestion cannot explain why the laws on either side of this one also prohibit kinds of mixing.

7. For this approach to fables see Richard F. Burton, *The Tale of a Thousand Nights and a Night*, terminal essay, 3A.

8. Herodotus 2.134.

9. Another relevant coded theme is that once animals were the same as humans: slaves (blacks) the same as owners.

10. "The Wonderful Tar-Baby Story."

11. "How Mr. Rabbit Was Too Sharp for Mr. Fox."

12. "Mr. Fox Is Again Victimized."

13. "Mr. Fox Is Outdone."

14. "Mr. Wolf Makes a Failure."

15. Aesop *Fabulae* 112.

16. Cf. Matthew 13.10ff.; Mark 4.10ff.

17. Cf. Matthew 21.33ff.; Mark 12.1ff.

18. Cf. Matthew 21.46; Mark 12.12.

19. See, e.g., George Fletcher, *A Crime of Self-Defense* (Chicago, 1988).

20. S. F. C. Milson, *Historical Foundations of the Common Law*, 2d ed. (Toronto, 1982), 232.

21. See, e.g., *Smith* v. *Brown and Cooper* 2 Salk 665 (1706).

22. See, e.g., Alan Watson, "Illogicality and Roman Slave Law," in *Legal Origins and Legal Change* (London, 1991), 251ff. at 253f.

23. This is a very simplified account: see A. W. B. Simpson, *A History of the Land Law*, 2d ed. (Oxford, 1986), 129ff.

24. See in general George L. Haskins, "Extending the Grasp of the Dead Hand: Reflections on the Origins of the Rule against Perpetuities," *University of Pennsylvania Law Review* 126 (1977): 19ff.

25. It has been suggested, by a friendly critic.

26. See M. E. Boismard, s.v. "Stephen" in *Anchor Bible Dictionary*, 6:208: "The primitive account of the martyrdom of Stephen is literally dependent on the narrative of the death of Naboth (Brodie, 1983). Beyond the historical facts, the author wanted to signify that Stephen's adversaries were not worth any more than the wicked Jezebel, whose memory had been held in disgrace by all Jews."

11 THE LOGIC OF STEPHEN'S SPEECH

1. God's covenant with Noah and his sons (Genesis 9.8ff.), however, imposed no obligation on them.

2. The version in Genesis 37.25ff. is rather different. Judah urged the other brothers to sell Joseph to the Ishmaelites, but it was some Midianite merchants who drew Joseph out of the pit and sold him to the Ishmaelites. In the account the terms *Ishmaelites* and *Midianites* seem to alternate: the Midianites sold Joseph in Egypt to Potiphar: Genesis 37.36.

3. Oddly, Scobie regards the speech as playing down the significance of the Holy Land: "Source Material," 405.

4. See, e.g., John Schultz, *The Chicago Conspiracy Trial*, 2d ed. (New York, 1993).

5. Another speech for the soul of the jury and nation is that of Andrew Hamilton in August 1735, defending John Peter Zenger against a charge of libel: see Leonard W. Levy, *Emergence of a Free Press* (New York, 1985), 37ff., and the literature that he cites, 38n. 79.

6. See, e.g., Josephus *War* 1.199; *Antiquities* 14.73, 18.35; cf. Emil Schürer, *The History of the Jewish People in the Age of Jesus Christ*, 2d ed., ed. Geza Vermes and Fergus Millar (Edinburgh, 1973), 1:243ff.

7. At *Antiquities* 15.5 Josephus claims Herod killed forty-five of Antigonus' most prominent supporters.

8. See, e.g., *Hus in Konstanz: Der Bericht des Peter von Mladoniowitz*, trans. Josef Bujnoch (Graz, 1963), 153ff.

9. The above account is written on the premise (that has to be taken into account) that the trial was a historical fact. If it was not, then the Romans had nothing to watch. Once again I wish to emphasize that Acts is the sole evidence for the trial of Stephen and the events surrounding it.

10. See, e.g., Richard J. Dillon in *New Jerome*, 741f.; Williams, *Acts*, 146 (who suggests Jesus may have stood to receive Stephen [premature?] or to plead his case in the heavenly court [why necessary?]); Williams, *Commentary*, 112 (who asks if this indicated Jesus' readiness to vindicate the innocent).

12 THE TRIALS OF JESUS AND STEPHEN

1. Richard J. Dillon in *New Jerome*, 740. See also Simon, *St. Stephen*, 20ff. H. P. Owen takes it for granted "that Luke wished to imply a correspondence between the death of Stephen and the death of Christ," "Stephen's Vision in Acts VII. 55–56," *New Testament Studies* 1 (1954–55): 224ff. This causes problems with the difference between καθημενος in Luke 22.69 and ἑστῶτα in Acts 7.56.

2. Mishnah Sanhedrin 5.5.

3. Indeed, for many Jews it would be a sacred duty not to pay the tax. Payment would be regarded as recognizing the Romans as rulers and as a breach of the command to have no ruler but God: Josephus *War* 2.118, 2.433, 7.253; *Antiquities* 18.4ff. This was the point behind the Pharisees' trick question to Jesus whether it was lawful to pay the Roman tax: Matthew 22.15ff.; Mark 12.13ff.; Luke 20.20ff.

4. Haenchen, for example, claims that Luke had the trial of Jesus in mind and used materials that were too dangerous for the first trial: *Acts*, 274.

13 PETER, STEPHEN'S SPEECH, AND PSALM 105

1. Peter's speech from Acts 3.12–16 is set out in chapter 1.

2. This term for Jesus appears only here, in Acts 22.14, and in James 5.6.

3. John S. Kselman and Michael L. Barré in *New Jerome*, 544.

4. I am following (with slight modifications) the translation of Lancelot C. L. Brenton, *The Septuagint with Apocrypha: Greek and English* (London, 1851), 761f.

14 SOURCE-CRITICISM

1. See, e.g., Trocmé, *Actes*, 188ff.

2. Haenchen, *Acts*, 272. A summary of modern scholarship will be found in Jacques Dupont, *The Sources of the Acts* (New York, 1964). Roloff is one of those who thinks Luke may have imposed the story of a trial upon a tradition of lynching: *Apostelgeschichte*, 111f., 126. For the absence of satisfactory results from source-criticism see, e.g., Wikenhauser, *Apostelgeschichte*, 11f.

3. Haenchen, *Acts*, 286ff.

4. Difficulties, not impossibility.

5. Bihler goes so far as to argue that the whole speech is by Luke: *Stephanusgeschichte*, 33ff. For Simon, it is "highly probable that the speech is, in its essentials, pre-Lucan": *St. Stephen*, 39; cf. Schneider, *Apostelgeschichte*, 447. For Bauernfeind, the speech could be a free composition by Luke, or he could have used earlier material for his own purposes: *Apostelgeschichte*, 111.

15 LUKE-ACTS AND THE STEPHEN AFFAIR

1. See, e.g., Joseph A. Fitzmyer, *The Gospel according to Luke I–IX* (Garden City, N.Y., 1981), 63ff.

2. Cf. David Daube, "Zukunftsmuzik: Some Desirable Lines of Exploration in the New Testament Field," *Bulletin of the John Rylands University Library of Manchester* 68 (1985): 53ff.

3. See, e.g., Alan Watson, "Leviticus in Mark: Jesus' Attitude to the Law," in *Unity, Purity and the Covenant: Reading Leviticus,* ed. John F. A. Sawyer (Sheffield, 1996).

4. It may be noted that Mark also shows a continual escalation of Jesus' hostility to the Pharisees, an escalation that is much less noticeable in Luke: see Watson, "Leviticus."

5. David Daube, *Civil Disobedience in Antiquity* (Edinburgh, 1972), 112ff. Daube cites the sources.

6. The Greek verb used is ἀρνέομαι 'to deny.' It is used at verse 69 and more especially also at verse 68 where it clearly refers to an evasion. There is no need to look for a different usage at 69.

7. I believe I owe this point to a conversation with Calum Carmichael.

8. We may note in passing that in Matthew 26.69ff. all three denials are public: the first is evasive and the second and third are direct. In John 18.25ff. all three denials are public and direct.

9. David Daube, "The Earliest Structure of the Gospels," *New Testament Studies* 5 (1958–59): 180f.; cf. Watson, *Trial*, 143ff.

10. See, above all, Daube, *New Testament*, 163ff.

11. But all four questions are in Matthew 22.15ff.

12. For discussion see Watson, *Trial*, 143ff.

13. See, e.g., Munck, *Acts*, 18f.; Conzelmann, *Acts* 20f.; Frederick F. Bruce, *The Acts of the Apostles* (Leicester, 1990), 126ff.; Haenchen, *Acts*, 181.

14. Isaiah 9.2ff., 11.1ff.; Jeremiah 23.5f., 33.14ff.; Ezekiel 34.23f., 37.24.

15. For the place of assembly see Strack-Billerbeck, *Kommentar*, 1:997ff.

16. See Robert J. Karris in *New Jerome*, 718.

17. Jerome Neyrey, *The Passion according to Luke* (New York, 1985), 71; quoted with approval by Karris in New Jerome, 718.

18. It is now completely unsurprising that I have made so little use of Jewish legal sources in this volume. For me, much of the Gospels of Mark and John are incomprehensible except against the background of Jewish law. The same cannot be said for Luke.

19. Cf. Barrett, *Acts*, 1:224f.

20. See Josephus *Antiquities* 18.26, 18.34.

21. On difficulties for the arrest and trial see, e.g., Haenchen, *Acts*, 214ff.; Conzelmann, *Acts*, 32ff.

22. Josephus *Antiquities* 20.97ff. For Wikenhauser, the Theudas of Josephus is not the Theudas of Gamaliel, who is someone who caused unrest after the death of Herod the Great in 4 B.C.: *Apostelgeschichte*, 76. There is no evidence for an earlier Theudas. See also Roloff, *Apostelgeschichte*, 104ff.; Schmithals, *Apostelgeschichte*, 61f.; Schneider, *Apostelgeschichte*, 400ff.; Barrett, *Acts*, 1:293f.

23. Josephus *Antiquities* 18.1ff., 18.23; *War* 2.433. See, as one among many modern commentators, Trocmé, *Actes*, 193.

24. See above all Haenchen, *Acts*, 257f. As one way out of the difficulties, J. W. Swain suggests the speech has been misplaced and should be in Acts 14: "Gamaliel's Speech and Caligula's Statue," *Harvard Theological Review* 37 (1944): 341ff. But he recognizes that this would not cure the anachronism or make the speech any less artificial.

25. Cf. Haenchen, *Acts*, 280; Bihler, *Stephanusgeschichte*, 48ff.

26. Scobie who does not seem to consider as a serious possibility that Luke could make mistakes sees here the importance of a Samaritan tradition: "Source Material," 407. I would discount any notion of strong Samaritan influence simply because of the emphasis on Jewishness in Stephen's speech. Scharlemann thinks Stephen was not himself a Samaritan, but his speech has some Samaritan characteristics: *Stephen*, 19f. See also Barrett, *Acts*, 1:350f.

27. Haenchen, *Acts*, 115f. For a discussion see also Wikenhauser, *Apostelgeschichte*, 14ff.

28. For an introduction to the problem, see now Michael Grant, *Greek and Roman Historians: Information and Misinformation* (London, 1995), 43ff., and the works he cites. With specific regard to Luke see Dibelius, *Studies*, 138ff.; Haenchen, *Acts*, 98ff.; Conzelmann, *Acts*, xliiiff.; Scharlemann, *Stephen*, 22ff.; Schmithals, *Apostelgeschichte*, 14ff.; Colin J. Hemer, *The Book of Acts in the Setting of Hellenistic History* (Winona Lake, Ind., 1990). Trocmé, *Actes*, 77ff. See also very generally Thomas Louis Brodie, "Greco-Roman Imitations of Texts as a Partial Guide to Luke's Use of Sources," in *Luke-Acts: New Perspectives from the Society of Biblical Literature Seminar*, ed. Charles H. Talbert (New York, 1984), 17ff.

29. The Latin text will be found in *Corpus Inscriptionum Latinarum*, vol. 13, no. 1668, col. 2; *Fontes Iuris Romani Antejustiniani*, 2d ed., ed. Salvatore Riccobono (Florence, 1941), 1:281ff. Convenient English translations of parts (also with the text of Tacitus) are in Naphtali Lewis and Meyer Reinhold, *Roman Civilization, Sourcebook II: The Empire*, 3d ed. (New York, 1990), 52ff.; Grant, *Historians*, 49ff.

30. Kenneth Wellesley, "Can You Trust Tacitus?" *Greece and Rome*, n.s., 1 (1954): 13, 29, 26.

31. Wellesley says: "Let us grant that Tacitus has understood and reproduced one or two of the more obvious points of the original": ibid., 26.

32. But one must add the Gospel of Thomas 71.

33. For the argument that Stephen was an isolated figure in the history of early Christianity see Marcel Simon, "Saint Stephen and the Jerusalem Temple," *Journal of Ecclesiastical History* 1 (1950): 127ff.

34. The declaration is missing from Luke.

35. It may be noticed, though, that in 9.43 Peter stays with a tanner. Because of their contact with animal corpses, tanners would be ritually unclean. Peter could not have been too concerned about the possibility of contamination.

36. Acts, 8.14f., 9.31, 10.28, 11.1f., 13.43, 13.46ff., 14.27, 15.1ff., 18.4, 18.6, 19.10f., 21.25, 21.28, 23.1ff., 25.8, 26.20.

37. In Luke 7.1ff. Jesus' curing of the centurion's son is represented as a special case: the centurion was worthy, for he had built a synagogue for the Jews. Nor is anything said in the episode about salvation for non-Jews. For a discussion see, e.g., Watson, *Law*, 82ff.

16 THE AFTERMATH

1. For these arguments see now in general Watson, *Trial*; *Law*.

2. See, e.g., Louis H. Feldman in Shanks, *Christianity*, 30ff.

3. For Jewish attitudes toward Gentiles see, e.g., Sanders, *Judaism*, 267ff., 295ff.

4. Simon stresses that Stephen was "an almost solitary figure among the leaders of the first Christian generation" and that his theological thought is "very personal" and "almost completely aberrant": *St. Stephen*, 98. Scharlemann considers it "extremely doubtful that Stephen had any kind of direct following": *Stephen*, 54. That during the persecution the apostles were not scattered "throughout the countryside of Judea and Samaria" (8.1) suggests that the apostles at least had little to fear. Hostility would seem to be directed more to some than to others.

✠

INDEX OF TEXTS

✠ ✠ ✠

2 APOCRYPHA

3 NEW TESTAMENT

4 CHRISTIAN APOCRYPHA

5 ESSENE SOURCES